THE WH

SOUL HEALING FOR
CHANGING TIMES

KATHARINA WEHRLI

Earthlit Press

Please Read

The views and methodologies expressed in this book are intended for educational purposes or personal development. They are in no way a substitute for medical or psychiatric attention. The author is not responsible for any damage occurring from lack of necessary professional health care.

First Edition

ISBN 0-9772869-0-8

Library of Congress Control Number: 2005933961

Published by Earthlit Press

Wayland, MA 01778

www.earthlit.com

Dedicated to

Paramahansa Yogananda, Swami Sri Yukteswar,

and to my teacher Jeffrey Wolf Green.

Contents

PART ONE: THE INTERPLAY BETWEEN SPIRIT AND MATTER

PART TWO: WORLD CYCLES

PART THREE: EVOLUTIONARY HEALING

Preface

In my healing work I found that clients often did not get better, despite physical methods, emotional therapy, mental counseling, and spiritual practice. None of these approaches sufficed in getting to the root of what ailed many of them. This is why my work with people motivated me to search for a combination of healing modalities that would include the emotional realm along with a conscious focus on the soul.

Eventually it became clear that the answer was found in the mindset with which we were approaching healing and wholeness, not in the specific methods themselves. When I began to change this approach, a new dynamic emerged. The timely perspective of evolutionary healing restructured the foundation of my own consciousness. With this shift things became truly exciting. I began to attract clients who were willing to change some of their primary outlook on life from within their own psyche. Those who were open and receptive to letting go of past conditioning benefited to a larger degree than previously imagined.

In the past years I have been working on fine tuning my understanding and healing skills in working with this new mindset. Of course it is not possible to help everyone, and most clients would not openly admit that they got nothing out of a session. I simply never heard from them again. Yet I also happened to run into one or the other person filed away in my "I could not help" folder. This has occurred a couple of times in the most peculiar situations and improbable places, such as a painfully long security check line at the airport and my local supermarket already emptied by the rabid crowd before a blizzard. There a familiar face suddenly appeared, eager to reconnect. I found out that in fact my work with these clients had been quite helpful. Needless to say, waiting at the airport suddenly became very interesting, and the bare supermarket at the eleventh hour had just what I was looking for after all.

Acknowledgments

I thank all those who helped me to persevere in my efforts to bring this project to completion. My foremost appreciation goes to my clients who put their trust in my healing and teaching practice. Without them I could not have come to the deeper understanding that motivated me to write this book. I am particularly grateful also to my editor Jean Anderson, my proofreader Caroline Bliss, and to Kathleen Valentine for the implementation of my cover design.

Katharina Wehrli, August 2005

Introduction

Writing about healing in these complex, enigmatic, and troublesome times is challenging. Today's dismal and often chaotic-looking circumstances are the ground for negative projections. One cannot help but wonder and worry about where it all will lead. The reason for wise decisions becomes apparent in the reality of changing times. This is reflected in the book title *The Why In The Road*, which signifies both the crucial crossroads to be faced in the process as well as the reason for the crossroads. It calls attention to the past decisions, present choices, and imminent consequences we are given a chance to ponder.

In addition to supplying the reader with a constructive outlook, this volume contributes spiritual material in a basic formation. The way the material is presented here allows the development of cognitive self-help skills in the area of spiritual and psychological understanding. The ability to fearlessly scrutinize and integrate the dark side of life facilitates deeper insights. There is no light without a shadow, and without conscious knowledge of the shadow there can be no true growth in life.

Evolutionary healing describes the change in human consciousness occurring on our planet now. It supplies an entirely new viewpoint based on the present, which includes an understanding of the past and to a certain degree also of the future. It is first concerned with the origins of a global and time-specific imbalance, and with the description and analysis of the resulting psychological and alchemical dysfunctions. Then it points a way out, and finally it supports and coaches those who desire to move beyond.

Anyone who is interested in healing, self-improvement, and personal development can use this practical perspective. When principles make rational and intuitive sense, when they speak to us on a gut and heart level, and when we find them reflected in our environment, we tend to grow with them. Over time they guide us in the direction most beneficial for us. Since in essence evolutionary healing is vast, culturally complex, deeply psychological, and spiritual, it may take time to become really graspable. Once assimilated, it fits smoothly into the personal toolbox of life skills.

Although not an in-depth study of history, psychology, anatomy and physiology, metaphysics, or astrology, the material originates from myriad sources. The outcome resembles a collage that creates a new picture, while using already-existing images. The intention in examining and expanding the perception and understanding of our time is to provide an overview of the bigger picture within the process of becoming (evolution). Thus the tension of past and future as experienced in the present can be understood from a truly revolutionary and empowering perspective.

The first part of the book establishes the foundation from an alchemical point of view. It supplies a cosmology of existence while exploring the interplay of spirit and matter from the perspective of reincarnation and the human soul. As one of the laws of the physical, astral, and causal planes, evolution is put into the context of the soul's motion from matter to spirit. The internal and external battles inherent in this process are seen within the world of complementary opposites.

The second part of the book deals with world cycles that explore human consciousness within a 26,000-year period of spiritual ascension and materialistic decline. Thus, we can comprehend the tension of past and future as experienced in the present in an unprecedented context. As much as healing is in the wound, we need to first examine this wound. In evolutionary healing the phenomenon of suffering is seen in its range from psychospiritual pathology to an inherent condition. Although suffering is a natural part of the human condition, unnecessary suffering is a disease that urgently needs a cure.

The third part of the book comprises an outlook on the future, and clearly describes the "Y" in the road that we face. If we can embrace the necessary changes, choosing the right fork in the road will bring gradual improvement. If not, cataclysmic change is unavoidable. Through metamorphosing our limitations, a shift in awareness takes place from adapted man-made paradigms toward natural principles. The essence of evolutionary healing is in the understanding of life as a supernatural mechanism moving from separation and diversity to attraction, unity, and oneness. In the final analysis it views healing as the refining motion from doubt to faith, matter to spirit, and involution or stagnation to evolution.

Even though historical facts and material from various sources are utilized in this writing, the emphasis is on a larger perspective. The boundaries are clear, but they do belong to a metaphysical framework. They set the tone for an interaction of the tangible and the elusive. Assimilation of the larger perspective to which this writing is dedicated takes some patience, an open mind, as well as reflection and observation.

In life and in healing, it is often not enough to analyze the various parts. Concentration on the whole is also needed to gain useful answers and definite direction. The practice of seeing, understanding, and consciously living life not only requires intelligence, but also a feeling of one's unfolding inner wisdom. Therefore, you are encouraged to let both your brain as well as your heart engage in this reading experience. The challenge lies in penetrating with the mental gaze beyond any preconceived notion and model. In bridging the distance between head and heart we receive the tools to know ourselves. They give us the strength to fight with fearlessness the battle of life and truth that is always worth fighting for. What could be more rewarding and useful?

Why are we here, why are the present circumstances so disheartening on a global level, what are our lessons, and how can we best deal with the challenges we face in our lives? These are some of the questions this book is trying to answer in a different way. Because the material is revolutionary, it is also challenging. It may very well metamorphose some of your own cognitive limitations relative to evolution, healing, and answers to some of the above questions.

PART ONE

THE INTERPLAY BETWEEN SPIRIT AND MATTER

1. Evolution

Evolution is a process of metamorphosing limitations on all levels in order to adapt to life's demands, situations, and circumstances in more proficient ways. Metamorphosis occurs for all life forms on this planet. It is different from transformation. When two opposite corners of a square are pushed closer together, the square turns into a diamond shape. The original shape is still recognizable, although it clearly has changed. This development exemplifies transformation. Metamorphosis on the other hand produces a completely new shape. The initial form has mutated, and no resemblance with the original configuration is left. An example is the caterpillar turning into a butterfly.

Metamorphosis clearly is more drastic than transformation. Both these progressions are necessary for adaptation to change, the only constant in life. When change is required to grow beyond limiting circumstances, metamorphosis through complete alteration is often the dynamic evolution chooses over transformation. There are two types of metamorphosis, one is slow and gradual, the other one is cataclysmic.

Nature demonstrates both types of modifications. Slow and gradual evolution is found in a seed on the ground. With the right conditions it germinates and grows into a tree. Now the original form of the seed can no longer be identified in the tree. A metamorphosis has taken place. It was not dramatic, but rather flowed smoothly from one stage to another.

Cataclysmic evolution is much more harsh and unsettling. It can also be devastatingly grievous and unfortunate. This type too starts out with a slow and gradual process, but there are no obvious signs of change. Even though these initial small shifts are practically undetectable, in this case they are the beginning of a process that builds on resistance. Pressure builds gradually but steadily. All of a sudden the point of no return is reached, and cataclysmic change becomes unavoidable. Volcano eruptions occur with such a dynamic, so do earthquakes and avalanches. Tidal waves and storms also build in a similar manner. Consequently, this also is a pattern intrinsic to life's natural unfolding.

Humans experience metamorphosis also as a psychological process. In every life there are intense times of stress that require us to fundamentally change our relationship to ourselves, to others, or to certain areas of our existence. If we did not change, we would no longer be able to function. However, human nature relies on habit and self-consistency. What we know and are used to makes us feel secure. Change therefore creates insecurity within the human psyche. The bigger the changes we need to make, the more our sense of familiarity and our habitual way of being and acting is threatened. It is this insecurity that tends to breed resistance to necessary change. The more we struggle to keep the status quo of an inner attitude, or some external conditions, the greater our resistance to necessary change will be.

By averting the issue at hand, change can be resisted for a limited amount of time. Because the force of evolution contains an intrinsic thrust, however, carrying on in the old familiar mode counteracts its direction. Just as with avalanches or volcanic eruptions, the pressure keeps building until it reaches the point of no return. This is when a more or less cataclysmic event occurs to ensure the necessary change. At that moment all control is lost, and we do not know why things are happening the way they are.

Never would we have purposely chosen such change! We may not even have known that we resisted that change. Now that it is happening seemingly of its own volition, there is no other way but to cope with it. In the future we may look back and understand the reasons for this tumultuous change. By then the metamorphosis will be complete, and something in our consciousness will be changed fundamentally along with it. Certain limitations are obliterated, new possibilities open up, and we possess new skills. This phenomenon will empower us to gain an expanded perspective leading to more suitable and personally relevant choices. Thus evolution occurs despite our initial resistance.

As mentioned above, metamorphosis can result also from slow but progressive change. Forming relationships with other people, an institution, or a body of knowledge is an example of non-cataclysmic evolution. Through forming a relationship with someone or something outside of ourselves, we take in new information and components we previously lacked. With this process a type of energetic osmosis takes place. For instance, we might enter a program or school in order to learn something new. We absorb the material taught in classes and through the required reading material. By the time we graduate our system has assimilated the new information, and we have gained a certain degree of confidence. We have also practiced the new skills, and are finally qualified to use all this by serving others. With practice the acquired new capacities will open doors to opportunities that otherwise would stay closed. Through schooling and training, limitations are metamorphosed, and our capacity to be helpful and resourceful to self and others evolves.

Another example for slow, progressive evolution is the process of getting to know another human being in an intimate way. Every intimate relationship allows us to learn new things about ourselves, about the way the other person sees the world and processes information, and about the limitless nature of creativity. When we spend time with someone we feel secure and connected with, we absorb some of this person's very way of being. Through this contact some of our own limitations are metamorphosed as well.

All of life's processes are subject to change. There is no permanence in any living organism. Some change slower, others change faster. Even a two thousand year old tree grows, ultimately reaches a state of completion, and dies. All living beings are forced to adjust to their environment. As they do, they utilize resources available to them, which transforms their limitations. Consequently, life is a dynamic of perpetual becoming and adjusting in the face of continuously changing circumstances. This is what makes life interesting and challenging.

It is important to understand life from a standpoint that includes the physical, mental, and emotional as well as spiritual realms of existence. In the context of these various planes we can contemplate the origin of this organic development we call life. What creates life and causes evolution? Who conducts the entire scenario and maintains balance? There is a force greater than what we can encompass with our rational mind. Human beings have learned to employ this force in various ways, and this has occurred in an accelerated fashion over the past couple of centuries. Using physics, chemistry and other sciences, Western culture has drawn upon the power of electricity, and other natural forces present in the universe. Force in and of itself, however, is not the cause of life. There is intelligence far greater than our own human intelligence, which I refer to as Universal Source. It is this intelligence that conducts all of earthly existence and the entire creation of solar systems, galaxies, and universes to work together harmoniously. The Universal Source orchestrates all of nature and the various forces in the cosmos.

The way we make use of science and technology has brought about massive global imbalance. It is exactly this intelligent, self-governing ability to harmonize the natural forces that is absent in our human technology. The limitations in this so-called modern progress lie in the defiant stance of not wanting to acknowledge anything beyond what we can confirm with our senses. In order to gain true insight into the workings of this universe, we need to further examine the notion of the Source. For now it will suffice to say that the Universal Source is the origin of all manifested things.

With human beings, the psychological and spiritual aspects play a major role in the evolutionary development of consciousness. These aspects are tied in with survival and reproduction. They also rely on innate, cultural and environmental factors such as genetic make up, race, gender, nationality, region, and family. Moreover, evolution of conscious awareness depends on the age of the individual. The genetic imprinting regarding the age of the organism is programmed to develop at a certain rate. During the first part of life the focus is on growth and expansion. With youth and up to middle age it seems as though life was a perpetual adventure continuing endlessly into the future, despite knowledge of the aging process. While curiosity peaks during childhood and adolescence, discovering new possibilities prevails as a major characteristic well into middle age. The physical aches and pains, or even minor restrictions imposed by an aging body are not normally confining or of any lasting concern. Only once this phase of life passes does the individual realize that time indeed is setting limitations on certain physical and energetic attributes that were previously taken for granted.

As the later years replace middle age, maintenance becomes the core of events. At a particular point people realize that there are limitations regarding the usefulness of their body. The still distant, but definite culmination of the intrinsic life span becomes then more conspicuously evident. Owing to the realization that life will end sooner rather than later, many people begin to focus their attention on what it is they really want. This accelerates the evolutionary pace in a natural way. As time seems to run out, issues that have not been addressed in earlier years become important. All of a sudden it is obvious that if they are not dealt with, they will never be resolved. Growth beyond these limitations now appears precious. Accordingly, the genetic programming of the natural aging process facilitates psychological and spiritual evolution.

2. How Spirit Matters

Spirit is absolute and perfect. In relation to creation, spirit is called God or Universal Source. This spiritual Source is cosmic consciousness, the infinite supreme intelligence that governs everything. In and of itself complete, and without needing to accomplish anything, this Source nevertheless had a desire to create tangible objects and beings. When the Source decided to generate the finite forms of the manifested creation, it divided itself into matter and consciousness. A dualistic universe was set in motion, in which all things are bound by the natural law of limitations. Within the manifested creation, however, the dynamic of evolution carries the potential to metamorphose all limitations. Evolution therefore is the dynamic that most closely resembles that ideal of perfection, or at least the movement toward perfection.

Essentially, every human being's consciousness has the potential to rise above dualistic limitations into the perfected state of ultimate realization and enlightenment. To concentrate on the infinite makes the mind unlimited. But under ordinary circumstances the mind is accustomed to perceive everything through the senses of the physical body. It relies on the information it receives through the senses, and trusts them implicitly as to the nature of reality. As long as consciousness is bound by the relativity of time and space in this way, it is impossible to reach perfection.

Whether we consider the Universal Source as belonging to one or the other gender is a question of speculation or rather, a philosophical distinction that is culturally conditioned. To relate to the Source in a more intimate way, human limitations tend to create a personal image in the form of a male or female figure. God or Goddess is spirit, so how could this be a restricted concept confined by relativity, or subject to dualities such as male and female? In and of itself the Source is absolute, ultimate, limitless, all pervading, metaphysical coercion. It is the origin of everything, encompassing all male and female life forms, as well as all psychological dynamics, including masculine and feminine. It is only natural then not to put a definite gender assignment on the Source. Still, God most often is seen as masculine, and referred to as "He."

The image many people connect with God is an intimidating male figure in the sky. He holds all the power, while judging with a set of rigid and unnatural rules from his lofty place of detachment. In our present time, as well as during the past several thousand years, the Source has been associated almost exclusively with the masculine principle. The feminine aspects of existence are considered unworthy of possessing divine attributes. Within the inscrutable laws of nature this notion is far from truth. For reasons to be examined in the chapters to follow, these views were nevertheless adopted as unquestionable beliefs. Hence, in addition to being confusing and very difficult to comprehend, God also has become one of the most unnatural concepts of all.

The manifested aspect of the Source is the natural creation. It consists of inert and living things such as nebulae, galaxies, black holes, white dwarves, solar systems, and planets. Earth, for instance has an atmosphere and also hosts a multitude of life forms. Although it takes very specific and rarely met conditions, it is more than likely that there are other planets in this, and in other galaxies that also host life forms.

In a more narrow sense we often call our planet Earth, with all her inhabitants including rocks and the weather, Mother Nature. She truly is the physical sustainer of all life. All of the other phenomena such as stars and galaxies, however, belong to the manifested creation as well. We can see the natural creation as feminine and female in its life-giving and life-bearing functions of receptive and nurturing qualities. Likewise, we can attribute masculine and male qualities to the life-generating principle with its energy moving out from the Source. Both biological genders are required for procreation, and both psychological dynamics take place in the manifestation of the natural creation. From this perspective it also appears wise not to limit creation to a gender specific category.

The supreme intelligence organizes planetary, interstellar and galactic movements. It regulates the seasons, enables the grass and the flowers to grow in the spring and the trees to lose their leaves in the fall. This cosmic force causes our heart to beat and our tears to flow when we are moved. Its supernatural consciousness governs processes of growth, decay, and healing. It is the abundant power behind all resources and the true significance in all things. The reason this supreme intelligence is also called the Source is because all things originate and return to it. In the end the manifested and the unmanifested aspects of the Source are like the dreamer and his or her dream. Essentially they are the same.

Considering the above points we could argue that God is both male as well as female and therefore should probably be referred to as "It." Using the non-gendered "It" will also alleviate the grammatical awkwardness in the text. Furthermore, because of the above-elaborated gender issues, as well as for simplicity's sake, in this writing the term "God" is used interchangeably with "Goddess." Furthermore, several expressions such as "Creator," "Source," "Divine," "Infinite," and "Great Spirit" are used as synonyms as well. As we will see later, gender assignment relative to the Source and its creation really has more to do with the fickleness of human intelligence, whose flag blows with the wind of convenience. The issue of gender can be a core issue only if we do not concentrate on the essential nature of the Universal Source and its creation. Yet an authentic comprehension of this Source is vital. It is not possible to observe its nature through the rational mind, but rather only through wisdom gained from intuitive perception.

True cosmic wisdom is insight regarding the Source's interplay with its manifested creation. Our intuitive faculty increases through regular meditation. This said, it seems futile to describe cosmological dynamics, except that a description will most likely help the reader understand the material presented here. This writing does not claim to be a complete guide relating the eternal truths of cosmic wisdom. Infinitely wiser and more comprehensive volumes on this subject are readily available. Even so, to explore the natural processes at work in the universe we must delve into a practical description of the interaction between spirit and matter. In this context the purpose of supplying metaphysical information is part of a red thread that connects darkness with light, question with answer, cause with effect, chaos with balance, involution with disease, and evolution with healing.

The descent of spirit into matter is the dynamic of involution, and the ascent from matter into spirit equals evolution. The interplay takes place on increasingly more subtle levels. Next to the physical plane, are the emotional, mental, psychological levels, and, at this point in time for many people also the energetic level. There are finer realms of existence still, just beyond the grasp of our senses. These metaphysical realms are still part of the manifested creation. Unless someone is born with the necessary extra sensory perception, however, comprehending such realms requires special spiritual training. To achieve the desired results, it may be necessary to prolong such training for many years, perhaps many lifetimes. All of creation exists within various frequencies of vibration. By training to intuit through the subtle planes of conscious awareness, we can perceive these vibratory frequencies as light or sound.

The astral world of luminous objects and beings such as devas, angels and spirit guides consists of subtler vibratory frequencies. Not all the astral world is pleasant, nor are all astral beings human benefactors. An even more astute level of the manifested creation is the causal realm of ideas that gives rise to the less subtle astral and the gross physical planes. We can compare the causal realm with the blueprint of a house. The architect designs the blueprint, which then becomes the reference point for all the workers involved in the construction of the building. Likewise, the causal plane contains the basics from which the astral and physical planes are mapped out. The Source is the architect. Regular human existence only takes into account the physical and a small percentage of the astral and the causal realms in form of emotions, thoughts, intelligence, and intuition. But whether we know it or not, the underlying dynamic is the interplay of these different realms with spirit.

Without spirit being the dynamic Source of this cosmic arena, there would be no play, or, to take again the above example, there would be no blueprint, no construction, and no house. However, the architect exists independently of it all. This is why God is greater and more powerful than anything or anyone else. Goddess perhaps decided to create these vibratory realms of existence in the desire to play the game of manifestation and consciousness. In any event, the interplay of spirit and matter was set in motion. In it the threefold force of creation, preservation, and dissolution controls manifestation. Where there was once no natural creation but only spirit, matter and beings are now formed, sustained and destroyed. On the premise of evolution and involution consciousness is activated and brought in line with matter.

Worlds emerge, evolve, collide, and disintegrate all in a seemingly random fashion. Hindu philosophy, for example, teaches about "days and nights of Brahman." The "days" pertain to vast periods of time where there are manifested universes in existence, and the "nights" refer to periods where the Universal Source rests from creating. Astronomers and astrophysicists do not know whether the universe is going to keep expanding forever, or whether there will be a point where it will all stabilize, or perhaps shrink again. All they know is that it has been expanding since what they call the "big bang." The point here is that in the finite reality of the manifested creation change is ever-present, sometimes in cycles of growth, sometimes in cycles of destruction. Even during cycles of evolution, however, the ultimate perfection is never reached. Since there can be no perfection in a manifested universe, the feature of returning to the Source is "programmed" into the creation. We will see how this expresses itself in the following chapters.

3. Reincarnations and the Soul

Human beings are born in different states, socially, physically, emotionally, mentally, and spiritually. The reason for these observed differences is unclear. Injustice is part of human existence even though it does not seem to make any rational sense. Why are some people healthy while others are born with physical or mental dysfunctions? Why should one person have all the money in the world and not use it wisely, while others do not have enough money to afford the education they desire, or yet others cannot even buy food, or clothing? Why are some children born into loving families, while others struggle to survive in physically, mentally, or sexually abusive homes? Examples for these differences and inequalities are numerous. Some injustices are so excruciatingly painful that we block them out to keep living our lives. From the perspective of "one life is all there is," there is really no satisfying explanation for unfairness.

When contemplating the concept of reincarnation, on the other hand, things become clearer. Rather than catering to the thought that we are all born with a clear slate, this idea opens up a perspective where past actions of good or bad quality have preceded the present life. Reincarnation generates a context within which individual differences do indeed make sense. From this point of view we can now consider the karmic law of cause and effect. Past life habits, frustrated desires, aversions or attractions to things or people, greed, selfishness, false pride, generosity, wisdom, foolishness, the effect of all past actions, and many more factors all play a role in our current circumstances. If reincarnation is valid, then there must be a vehicle that carries all our highly individualized information. This vehicle or medium must be of a quality that transcends the boundaries of time and space, while concurrently possessing the memory and storage capacity of a very accurate and immense data bank. This is where the notion of the soul comes into play.

It is not possible to fathom the soul with a mind accustomed to obeying outer sensory impressions to the exclusion of all else. Understanding this concept requires a discriminating intellect that embraces eternal truths. The intellect is receptive to intuitive wisdom above and beyond sheer deductive reasoning, which is only functional on the plane of relativity. Deductive thinking in the end is always confined within the narrowness of logic, and therefore also is subject to false reasoning and delusion. The human mind falls prey to the ever-changing impressions of the senses and the finite world of matter. Within these parameters it is used to measure and compare all impressions and responses.

Intuition, on the other hand, can grasp timeless ideas. An open mind with focusing power and depth to behold the true nature of things must balance inference. To perceive the transcendent reality underlying the world of matter, the mind must be trained. Then it will be able to hold the charge of an increasingly more powerful intuition. This is a gradual process, but ultimately the mind becomes stabilized in intuition beyond comparing and rational thinking. To a mind rooted in the infinite light of truth, the concept of the soul is intrinsically practical and cherished.

The Universal Source fashioned souls as part of the manifested creation. The soul is the indestructible core of a person. It is not the body, mind, or emotional content, but rather the consciousness that gives rise to all of these. The soul is an energetic entity that merely changes form. Intuitive soul perception facilitates and guides all actions for the highest good of a person. For most of us who do not possess these attributes of perception described above, however, the soul remains entirely unconscious. We make our decisions based on identification with our personality. Every incarnate soul creates an ego with a personality. Without the ego people would not be able to experience and know themselves as separate entities that have a distinctly personal earthly experience. Yet the ego is not the core of human existence, the soul is.

Knowing itself to be infinite, the soul without its human attributes lacks earthly survival mechanisms. Then again, the ego has no awareness of the infinite realm. The intermediary that links the two complementary forces is the psyche. Thus one cannot act without the other's conscious or subconscious knowing. The psyche is the soul's consciousness expressed through the ego. It is involved with the individual's physical and emotional survival struggles. The psyche takes care of important aspects the soul would otherwise neglect. Likewise, without the psyche, the ego would let the soul fall by the wayside. In this arrangement the soul continues to give us hints of its true desires and intentions for our lives, but more often than not these hints are experienced as mere sticks between the spokes. When inexplicable obstructions within our own psyche puzzle us, we fail to understand the intuitive language of the soul. All too often we prefer to concentrate and act upon our conscious worldly ego-driven desires.

Earthbound existence causes human consciousness to forget about its true and timeless nature. The soul identified with the ego perceives what is needed within the circumstantial parameters of one life. Through the body and its senses the psyche perceives only the finite world of matter. It is therefore compelled to act according to worldly needs and their resulting desires. These desires can easily lead to actions that are inherently wrong. They leave a mark of imbalance or negative karma in the universe. The consequences of these wrong actions are carried forward with the soul into future lifetimes. Hence, next to positive characteristics, the personality of virtually every human being develops faults and wrong character traits. They dictate that things need to be worked out at some future point.

The essence of the soul, however, is just as incorruptible as it is immortal. Its true essence is capable of realizing its immortal, Goddess-like and Goddess-given qualities. Through its immutable consciousness the soul also possesses inherent knowledge of all individual past life experiences. To rise above the accumulated negative tendencies that solidified into bad habits and faulty attributes, the soul chooses circumstances that allow it to work them out. Each incarnation is the continuation of the previous life story. Thus, the evolutionary path is a journey with many chapters. The previous chapters are held in the subconscious memory banks and in the cellular memory throughout the body. They influence people in their present experiences and in the outlook toward the future. To grow beyond the limitations of the past, everyone is in a perpetual state of becoming. Depending on the amount of resistance or cooperation relative to the lessons at hand, this evolutionary process sometimes is forceful or even cataclysmic, at other times steady, gradual, and gentle.

Where does the soul go after death, and how does it return into the form of another human body? As we have seen in the previous chapter, the manifested creation consists of various levels or realms of finer or denser quality. They are the vibratory frequencies of the material, the astral, and the causal universes. Upon physical death the soul leaves the human body. It also leaves the psyche, ego and personality behind. The soul then enters the astral world. In this world it meets up with other souls it interacted with during other earthly incarnations or other astral sojourns. It also encounters higher astral beings whose energies are harmonious and whose wisdom is soothing. For a soul who lived a sincere, responsible, and conscientious earthly life, the astral world can be a time of rest and peace, sometimes also a time to learn higher lessons. If on the other hand an individual has lived a wicked or corrupt earthly existence, upon passing the soul will go to astral hell. There, the inherent conscience of the soul is tortured by the memories and consequences of its malevolent earthly deeds.

It often does not take long before such a soul is incarnated back into a body to work out some of this accumulated negative karma.

Most souls in between earthly lives do not ascend all the way to the causal realm, which requires higher degrees of evolution to roam in. Thus, for most souls physical death is astral birth and vice versa. During an astral sojourn a soul awaits the right karmic and evolutionary conditions for its next incarnation in a physical body. When these conditions present themselves, the soul will once more resume an earthly existence. All the above processes take place in the manifested creation. Although astral and causal universes are not a conscious perception for most people, they are by no means beyond specific laws that rule these realms. In other words, they also are part of the manifested universe.

As the soul progresses over a series of many, many lifetimes, the personalities it creates become increasingly more aware of their own inner nature and purpose. To advance beyond the limitations imposed by pre and postnatal errors, it is important to use determination. The Indian saint Patanjali taught that all human souls were made in the image of Goddess, and were sent to Earth for the purpose of enjoying the goodness of life. But by forming likes and dislikes, human beings became attached to what they felt and experienced. This attachment created a compulsion.

In order to maintain the desired conditions, people began to act against their own better judgment. Thus the necessity to work out the karma of past wrong actions perpetually generates incarnation after incarnation.

Every soul's true nature is the enjoyment of eternal wisdom. It is only through the identification with earthly living and the natural attachment to sensory impressions that human beings have forgotten their true origin. Each soul is an individual aspect of cosmic consciousness beyond the manifested creation. Encased in a body it has a twofold nature. Finite, as well as infinite, the soul belongs to both, the natural creation and the eternal unmanifested spirit. The finite aspect of the soul is the ego consciousness. Over many lifetimes we become more aware of the quality and intentions that fuel our actions. We also learn to be honest with ourselves in the realm of feelings, and therefore become more attuned to our inner nature and purpose. Psychological awareness and healing work is an important part in this emotional learning experience.

Emotional work generates awareness of ego-based impulses. The psyche learns to sort out the constructive from the destructive impulse. Rather than merely acting on ego-based impulse, it becomes skilled at consistently making the right choices. This leads to continuously positive action, which in turn carries good karma. Alignment with eternal truths brings about spiritual awareness of our infinite nature. As this process unfolds, the psyche begins to pay attention to the soul's call. This is an expansive sense, which is quite enjoyable, even blissful. Eventually we learn to seek this soul happiness unremittingly. Until we achieve this state permanently, incarnations continue to be our terrestrial playground and evolutionary work environment.

It is said in the Hindu scriptures that attainment of liberation from earthly incarnations takes a million years when a soul follows the path of right action. However, repeated resistance and negative karma double this time. With the right use of meditation, yoga, and other spiritual disciplines that contain the eternal truths leading to liberation, the path may be shortened dramatically. In this process, discrimination and adherence to right action continue to be required attributes. Whatever the chosen sacred techniques may be, it is essential to follow their practice faithfully and consistently. Only a few are capable of walking on this path, as it takes constant mindful concentration, total commitment, and unwavering faith in the face of contradictions, setbacks, and unexpected hardship. This is why there are so few self-realized individuals.

For most people the struggle of ordinary existence fully preoccupies their consciousness. Being bogged down by a thousand perpetual loose ends, the worldly aspects of their lives require all their attention. When they finally get a break, they are too tired to invest additional energy into reaching for what seems to be a vague and intangible spiritual goal. In desperate need for rest, most people seek to recuperate through the same material channels as the main part of their busy lives takes place. They relax through the worldly medium of outer sense gratifications. It is always easier to go downhill on a wide road than it is to walk uphill on a narrow and precipitous path toward a seemingly uncertain goal. Therefore, evolution remains long and challenging for most souls.

At this point in time a growing segment of the population is open and willing to devote some time to the pursuit of a spiritual goal and practice. These people advance more rapidly on their evolutionary journey. But even those who balance right action with periods of spiritual attunement often miss certain developmental aspects in their practice. They do not understand or follow some part of the path incorrectly, which leads to the necessity of further earthly incarnations.

There are many wise men and women whose lives have reached a high degree of intuitive power, but they are still living earthly lives. Perhaps they were born into a family or have children of their own who teach them through direct experience to gain those very attributes they have omitted in the past. Some share their lives with a partner with whom they have some karma of past wrong action that now is being worked out through the relationship. Others reap the good karma of being with a true soul mate. Their spiritual progress is the fruit of their commitment to each other, and to the path they have in common.

Not all souls were created at the same time, thus the "age" of any individual soul also plays a role in the level of development it has attained. The act of consciously seeking liberation applies only to those who have achieved a relatively high degree of experience, knowledge and wisdom. For them the "burn out" of many earthly lifetimes expresses itself in saturation or even boredom with mundane living. Conversely, for most people the effort to know the Source is easily thwarted by worldly interests that still hold a relatively high degree of fascination. Amusement, curiosity, and sense bound impulses are usually too strong to allow for the serious quest of fast spiritual evolution.

The butterfly's struggle to break through the chrysalis allows it to develop necessary strength. Without this great exertion it could not fly. It is the strength gained in the effort that determines the butterfly's readiness for its final metamorphosis. Likewise, on the evolutionary path it is the attempt that matters, not the end result. The strength gained in this process will in the end bring the desired results. Spiritual as well as true worldly success is always measured by the degree of sincerity and determination to persevere in the face of setbacks, distractions, and lack of drastic or even slight improvements. Whoever consciously undertakes the spiritual tasks of integrity and kindness will advance on the evolutionary journey. This individual is developing the spiritual muscle to eventually reach the final destination of enlightenment.

The pain of disillusionment that earthbound living sooner or later presents often fuels those who do persevere on their journey. Over many lifetimes the yearning for the peaceful calm of infinite bliss becomes stronger than the endless tug of war pulling on the chain of worldly excitement and disappointment. Ultimately no mortal being really ever wanted to be created. Thus, the path to enlightenment is the grace the Goddess gives to all human beings to dodge the imperfection of the wheel of life. Since the manifested creation is an invention of the Source, it is only fair that we, who are made in the image of the Great Spirit, should have a way to break free from the creation and merge with what created us. The soul is this infinite image within each human being. When we learn to identify with the soul rather than with the ego, we are on our way to liberation. This liberation is the human mastery of the interplay between spirit and matter.

4. Desire

Desire is the driving force behind our actions. The kind of desires we have determines what we do. Desires originate in the soul from where they spur our willpower and determination. There are two types of desires in all human beings. The first one is the desire to individuate, to be a creature autonomous and separate from everyone and everything else. All earthly desires fall into this category. The other desire is complementary to earthly desires. It is the desire to merge with what originally created us.

On its evolutionary journey the soul pursues its desires in a dual motion pattern of separation from and returning to the Source. We all have an impulse to be whole, and an impulse to be an individual. People who are in a relationship still have a need to be on their own from time to time. They long to do something just for and by themselves. This is an example for those two balancing desires. The fact that the person still wants to be in the relationship signifies the impulse or desire to become perfected through merging his or her resources with something larger outside the self, in this case the partner. Assimilating these resources allows the individual to become more complete. The wish to be or do things separately symbolizes the urge to individuate. Discovering new territory to accrue further knowledge and develop new skills through independent development fulfills desires that lead to personal evolution.

All desires create attachments, resulting in even more desires that need to be satisfied. Satisfying them generates experiences, adds proficiency, and augments wisdom. Thus evolution can proceed. While gathering knowledge and experience, the individual learns to make better choices and to advance in an array of skills. It is a journey that takes a great many lifetimes, but inevitably leads to increasing insight and revelation relative to the true nature and meaning of life. As mentioned in the last chapter, the soul eventually grows tired of its earthly desires and the attachments those desires create. The curiosity to explore life has been satisfied. A sense of "Been there, done that" accompanies much of what worldly adventures have to offer. The psyche knows the outcome of most circumstances and therefore no longer wishes to repeat experiences of which it already has the inner knowing.

Desire

Fulfillment of a separating desire produces an instant sense of satisfaction. Buying a house or the dream car, building a business and becoming materially successful, or starting a new relationship, are all examples of such desires that bring a sense of accomplishment and fulfillment. Yet sooner or later this feeling of contentment wears off and is replaced with another one. This is a vague, nagging mood of dissatisfaction that compels the individual to search for more. He or she may think: "Great, what's next?" Some people continue to cater to their senses and powerful desires by buying a bigger house, a more expensive car, by building a more powerful business, or by entering another relationship. It is easy to fall prey to the attachment to such desires. Nevertheless, every time a desire is fulfilled the actual emotional state sooner or later will flip from satisfaction to discontent. The comfortable mood of gratification is replaced by a nagging sense of frustration.

This emotional state prompts us to look for more through the psychological attachment to peripheral desires. We will never find permanent contentment, however, through the fulfillment of any earthly desire. In essence, the automatic switch from fulfillment to dissatisfaction represents our soul's longing to be reunited with the Source. This desire to merge with the Universal Source is the transcendent spiritualizing impulse in all of us. Desires and the attachment to those desires are metaphysical baits that eventually lure the soul from the world of separation in diversity to unity with spirit. What we unconsciously and ultimately search for is soul fulfillment. When nothing else is satisfying, longing to merge with the Source becomes stronger. Over a great length of time more and more earthly desires are eliminated, until finally we make a conscious decision to search for transcendent, everlasting happiness in spiritual union with Goddess. Once we are able to experience some of this supreme reality, fulfillment is far greater than any previous gratification of world inclined desires. This is the incentive to follow the route to spirit, which is the deepest desire in every soul.

As human beings we are able to pursue only those desires of which we are conscious. Since the soul is not conscious to most of us, we are not aware of all our desires. Those desires that stay in the subconscious nevertheless have an effect on us. When we act in ways that do not move us in the direction of fulfilling the urgent soul desires we are unaware of, we are likely to experience circumstances or events that are shocking or otherwise disharmonious. Only much later do we understand why something like this may have needed to occur. It is the soul who determines the evolutionary pace, and when our ego consciousness does not collaborate with this, the soul programs events that will enforce the necessary changes. With this perspective it becomes possible to realize ahead of time when we need to change our situation; let go, move on, or whatever the necessary change may be, thus avoiding further cataclysmic events.

When we realize soul-based desires, evolution takes place gradually. Ego-based desires keep a person in a perpetuate loop of sense attachments, stale habits, pleasure seeking, or greed. The key point is to fulfill only those desires that are based in soul progress. How can we know whether a desire is based in the soul? These are the hunches, the inner voices, the interests and callings we often cannot explain or put in proper context. If they keep occurring, we need to pay attention. This allows us to realize that an urgent soul desire is trying to catch our attention. Instead of investigating, many of us decide to resist such soul calls. It seems safer and much more comfortable to keep going in the old familiar ways. This is how we get stuck in a rut. Once the soul's desire has grown strong enough, it will create the necessary pressure to change our reality. The soul is the driving force behind our personality. Whenever we resist this force beyond its tolerable threshold, we bear the consequences. In this framework it also is crucial to understand that suppressing any desires rooted in the psyche is not a viable option. Thus, no shortcuts are possible through denial or repression. As long as such desires consciously or subconsciously are present, we need to fulfill them within the parameters of right action and respectful attitude. Whatever wants, aspirations, or longings we suppress will become distorted, finding their outlet and expression through imbalance, complexes, compulsive behavior, addiction, rage, secret obsession, and so on.

Frequently the reason for denial or suppression is one of psychological and sometimes even physical survival. For fear or guilt we may suppress our emotional reality subconsciously. In this case the issues related to denial or suppression first need to become conscious. More often than not this only happens through the experience of some blockage, or through some cataclysmic event. We then finally realize the previously suppressed desires and can move toward fulfilling them.

The scandals around the Catholic Church and its pedophile perpetrators illustrate the futility of attempting to suppress natural earthly desires. The priests are obliged to take a vow of celibacy. Some truly live in inner peace and natural balance, but for most of them celibacy is not a natural state of being. It takes a very high degree of spiritual evolution before anyone is naturally celibate. Most people, including priests, obviously do not fit this category, nor should they. The truth is that demanding celibacy of these individuals is not only unrealistic but also inhumane. Such expectations force the priests to suppress their natural sexual being. If their desire to know and serve God is strong enough, then they are willing to suppress this aspect of themselves. This sets in motion a subconscious dynamic of distortion.

How the individual handles the repressed energy depends on their psychological makeup. Sadly, a few exhibit pedophile behavior. Others may have secret sexual relationships with adults, and some might be deeply unhappy and sarcastic. As a result of the unhealthy residual tension latent in their system, even others may become compulsive smokers or contract a serious disease. For some of these priests the results of their suppressed sexual desires lead to cataclysmic life experiences, which ensure that they devote their energy to looking at the root cause of the dysfunction. Awareness of priest sexual abuse is collectively increasing because now the truth of many unnatural dynamics is being revealed globally.

Perceiving one's past and present life experiences from the standpoint of the soul's desires and longings grants an expanded viewpoint. In addition, acknowledging desires from this deep perspective requires a particular type of responsibility. It is the responsibility that ultimately we are all accountable for the realities we create and experience. There are no coincidences, but rather spurred desires leading to specific actions, which result in specific effects. Therefore, particular situations we experience are the consequences of prior desires and actions. Benevolent desires lead to considerate and kind actions, which in turn create favorable circumstances. Greedy desires cause the individual to act selfishly, which results in unfortunate, difficult, or degenerate conditions.

As stated before, over the course of numerous lifetimes the desire to be one with the Source becomes progressively more emphasized. Only when all separating desires have been met can the soul reunite with the Source. The path to merging with Goddess leads over the choice of a spiritual path that is connected to actual experience, rather than boxed in with dogmatic rules. Ultimately, the desire to know the Source is complementary to all other desires. The less we wish to dwell in the world of external pleasure, and the more we strive to know the Source, the closer we get to attaining the priority to be united with the Source. Once our wish to consciously aspire to the Source, and to be united with it is firmly established, the scale at some point tips towards the permanent realization of this oneness. This then is the completion of the soul's evolutionary journey.

Because there is no division between their identity and that of the Source, self-realized people do only what they know pleases God. Once all separating desires have been fulfilled, the need to be an autonomous entity becomes obsolete. Since consciousness is no longer identified with the finite reality of the body and the external senses, there is no egocentric consideration left. When one merges with the Source there is no experience of separation and no necessity for a manifest existence in an individual life form.

Many souls who have completed their evolutionary journey nevertheless continue to be engaged in earthly lives. This is because they genuinely wish to help others by being a living illustration of the ageless wisdom they embody. A saint, or any other liberated soul teaches through direct experience. Such people serve as timeless role models for regular people, as Jesus or Krishna and many others have done.

5. Free Choice

Life's deeper purpose is the completion of the soul's evolutionary journey through fulfilling and eliminating all earthly desires. This journey can be smooth and pleasant, but most of the time it rather resembles a battlefield. Many people become so engrossed in this battle, they lack a definite direction on their path. For them the meaning of life is in taking care of immediate survival issues and in trying to enjoy life whenever an opportunity presents itself. Ultimate enlightenment or liberation may sound nice, but it remains a fleeting thought at best. Regardless of whether a person pursues a spiritual path or not, to keep focus on the immediate tasks at hand is important. Confusion starts where the right choice is muddled up by an array of contradictory desires. For those who try, clarity is still in reach. Making good choices in this light simply becomes the focal point. If right choices can be made consistently, progress on the evolutionary path is self-operating.

Every soul in a human body is an individual, separate entity. Along with this comes the freedom to choose. Because choices are not always clear cut, nor easy to make, this is both a blessing and a curse. The opportunity to choose between what is convenient or pleasant and what is right presents itself soon enough. Rather than simply doing the right thing there is a conflicting element of temptation to choose according to one's likes and dislikes. No matter how much we see what the right decision would be, we often give in to more ego-based desires of acting according to what we are most attracted to or compelled to do. Moreover, in order to feel secure and to have self-consistency, many choices instinctively seem natural, even if in fact they are not good choices. Therefore, what appears to be free choice can be conditioned by security needs and compulsion, or it may be influenced by greed and temptation. Every action has a reaction, and every choice has a consequence. The better the choices we make, the greater the freedom to move past limitations and redundant conditions.

Persuasion or compulsion never accomplishes evolution. It is the application of free will that accelerates growth. Strengthening this inherent free will is an important factor in the process of evolution. A wish is a disabled desire of the mind. Desire is a stronger wish that leads to sporadic efforts to propel itself into action. Determination is a desire powerfully directed towards the attainment of an objective. Then again, it is often daunted after a couple of fruitless attempts. Volition on the other hand is the continuous effort of determined, ceaseless actions directed at the accomplishment of a desire. It eventually becomes dynamic enough to produce the intended results. Therefore, the fulfillment of a specific desire is dependent on the strength and focus of a person's willpower to persevere.

Anyone can continuously repeat fulfilling the same ego based desires. This may be pleasurable, but it also can be a condition of inertia that blocks evolution. Such primal random will is doomed to stagnation, which eventually results in dysfunction and disease. The overeater, the compulsive adulterer, and the alcoholic are extreme examples. What is absent is the freedom to use determination in accordance with better judgment. Rather than directing their willpower toward thoughts that create truth and happiness, the people in the above examples indulge in sense gratifications that lead to misery and pain for themselves and others.

The moth is attracted to the light and burns in the candle flame because it does not know how to keep a safe distance.

Likewise, one or several senses can consume human beings. There is a difference between enjoying life and being compelled to experience pleasure. Humans are meant to enjoy themselves, but attachment to primal sense gratification boosts indiscriminate use of willpower. Thus the individual is easily lured into the trap of habitual indulgence leading to addiction. The temptation to repeat the experience is a compelling, pleasure-seeking thought that generates more destructive actions. Once caught in this self-perpetuating loop, the person falls prey to unfavorable states such as stagnation and addiction. These in turn lead to decay and finally to disease.

Because the evolution of willpower is vital in making consistently right choices, improving this inherently powerful human resource is useful. The following is a description of its various developmental stages. The randomness of the unrestrained and ungoverned willpower wastes energy and higher potentialities on temptations, passions, and immediate sense gratifications. It is very important to discern the destructive effects of random willpower, which is volatile, not regulated by wisdom and without any real purpose. Once this awareness is generated, we can recognize and objectify random willpower. This analytical process is constructive because it guides people to reason after the fact. Learning in hindsight is more likely to produce resistance to the tendency of falling prey to random will. It facilitates the next developmental stage. Through reflection random will is strengthened toward the thinking will of considered action. The thinking will is under the conscious control of the individual.

Through its inherent magnetic power a strong will generates direction that accomplishes its purpose. The innate dynamic force of willpower activates subtle vibrations in the universe. This compels the natural principles that govern life to respond to these positive vibratory frequencies. They create favorable circumstances in the person's immediate environment. This dynamic explains why praying with deep concentration is effective. Habitual actions that no longer suit the original purpose or goal weaken the thinking will. Discrimination also is necessary to maintain the strength of this type of willpower. Otherwise, the misguided will is out of alignment with the natural life governing principles, and therefore can no longer produce the desired results. It is then important to investigate how the goal or purpose was lost. Once this is clear we can redirect the will toward a suitable purpose that is in tune with the universal flow of energy.

Willpower derives its greatest strength from sincere intention, seeking the truth, as well as from aligning with harmonious actions beneficial to all beings and to life in general. Such a will never weakens; it leads to success through perseverance. This kind of willpower invariably finds a way because it is aligned with the natural laws of the universe.

Our human will is limited by the confines of the individual's personality and by the boundaries of the physical universe. Yet the will of the Source is limitless. When we are able to keep our focused willpower ceaselessly centered on commendable desires, it eventually becomes one with divine will. This dynamic divine will is already within our possession. It does not need to be acquired from scratch. All that is required is learning how to align our personal will with the divine will. Adherence to good principles through consistent practice strengthens this type of will.

The evolution of personal willpower is effective in facilitating conscious choices. Choosing correctly is the test all mortals are subjected to in order to show their devotional love. The Source granted human beings free choice for the purpose of sovereignty and autonomous actions. Because of this power to choose freely, the path to final liberation from earthly living is long and arduous. It is only thanks to the saints and sages who have reached a state of complete loving compassion that humanity even has a perspective on this path. When we are able to receive their teachings and guidance with an open heart, we begin to direct our free will toward the actions that produce further soul progress.

Enjoyment develops into spiritual bliss. Eventually right action and good choices become second nature. This is not due to an outer demand, but because of an inner sense of wanting to experience this type of fulfillment.

When loyalty and devotional love have been demonstrated sufficiently, God's compassion may permit a person to enter the state of permanent cosmic oneness beyond a manifested existence. Then, and only then will the battle of right choice making cease to be waged. Human volition without the grace of the Creator will not bring this final result. Regardless of how much a person's willpower is focused on the goal, without Goddess' compassion there is no liberation. Consequently, compassionate love is the ultimate power and liberating force in the universe. If we care to receive it, we are asked to give it. This graceful action is what the saints, sages, and other enlightened beings demonstrate through their legendary lives of devotion and selfless service. They have proven that the desire to be one with the Source needs to be practical. Without walking this path it is not possible to get to the destination. No matter how many separating desires may still be present, love and compassion speed up the soul's evolution. This further demonstrates that lofty spiritual ideas are yet another separating desire. Without their practical application they mean nothing.

6. Karma

Karma is the universal law of action and reaction. Its blind justice works with precision regardless of time in its linear direction of past, present, and future. Any action performed with lack of pure intention or against natural principles produces a delusive, erroneous, and discordant vibration. The law of karma sooner or later reflects that same vibration back to the soul, who in the meantime already may be incarnated in a new body and faced with entirely different conditions. Most likely this soul has long forgotten that it once acted in ignorance of eternal truths and thus transgressed against nature's principles. The personality this soul has adopted in its new life is oblivious to the fact that the current unpleasant circumstances are karmic dues to be worked out. The same is true for kind, benevolent, and ethical actions. They too produce vibrations that are sooner or later reflected back to the individual in a beneficial way.

Actions record in the subconscious mind with a tendency for repetition. Before we know it a new habit is formed and firmly embedded in the subconscious mind. This feature is helpful and saves time, so we do not constantly have to relearn how to perform our daily tasks and duties. But for this same reason it is also hard to break an unwanted or destructive habit. Sometimes an action does not immediately translate into a habit. Yet, since it did take place, it nevertheless leaves a trace in our subconscious mind. Thus, it easily develops into a habit at some later point. Depending on the nature of the initial action, it will be a beneficial or a destructive habit.

There are several distinctly different types of karma. The first one is free choice. As previously discussed, free choice does not necessarily guarantee right action. Its only condition is that it is made autonomously. Therefore, free choice is solely dependent on the values and qualities of the person who makes the choices. Whatever they may be, these choices result in future beneficial or adverse reactions. No other conditioning factor is attached to this form of karma. This is the only form of action where the power to sow the good seeds of beneficial circumstances or the malevolent seeds of misfortune is fully in the individual's hands.

The second kind of karma is the result of past life action. The body with its strong and weak tendencies, all present circumstances such as family, economic conditions one was born into, as well as success or lack thereof belong into this category of karma. At certain junctures opportunities that are clearly fated to occur present themselves. By the same token, misfortune can also strike seemingly out of the blue. When a beneficial situation presents itself we hardly ask: "Why is this happening to me?" Then again, this is exactly what we ask when we encounter a mishap. Rarely do we realize that our own past actions are associated with this. At some point a transgression against a natural principle occurred and set a discordant vibration into motion. Through the exacting justice of the universal law of cause and effect we are then subjected to an unpleasant, perhaps even painful experience at some later point in time. If instead of accepting responsibility we tend to feel victimized, we fail once more to honor the natural code. This leads to more disharmonious vibrations. If on the other hand we can cooperate fully with the circumstances, good karma will erase the adversity, and in turn result in future beneficial circumstances.

Another karmic cast is future tendencies waiting to manifest. Just as in the former category, they are the cause of past life actions. Their concealed potential is waiting to find an outlet. These actions are merely in the process of gaining momentum. Yet, at some future point they are certain to manifest. Depending upon the quality of the past actions they are based on, their manifestation can be beneficial or detrimental.

The last portion of karma is action performed from intuitive realizations. This is the finest and most evolved type of action. Its wisdom burns past action and therefore cuts karmic ties. This kind of karma does not initiate a future chain of action. The intuitive actions rooted in true wisdom are performed with the realization of unity with the Source. Since these actions are not spurred by separating desires or by any psychological attachment, the only gain associated with them is to please the Source. The motivating desire is to be aligned with the will of God in selfless service.

There are two distinct phenomena intrinsic to negative karma that need further definition. The first one is karmic retribution; the second one is evolutionary necessity. Both cases produce prohibiting circumstances such as failure, setback, afflicted relationships, or experience of abuse, loss, abandonment, betrayal, or violation of trust. The individual experiences all or some of this as physical, worldly, emotional, mental, or spiritual limitations. It is as though the hand of fate were holding these people down, not allowing them to stride toward good results. The reason for this experience is either karmic retribution or evolutionary necessity.

Karma

Wrong action large or small is action out of harmony with the natural life governing laws of the manifested universe. Whenever a person acts against these natural principles, the inherent wisdom of the soul programs a counter-effect that at some future juncture forces the individual to experience the consequences of these wrong actions. The law of karma necessitates a reaction to balance the vibratory frequencies. Therefore, understanding karmic retribution can be of real value and for some people also a great relief. It teaches through natural law that the consequences of past actions need to be compensated for. Taking personal responsibility for the current circumstances completes karmic retribution, and far more favorable conditions will replace the present difficulties in the future.

What metamorphoses the outlook is not so much knowing that the mortifying conditions will lift at some point, as it is the ability to surrender to them. The ego faces limitations imposed by the law of karma. Letting go into the insurmountable obstacle of this experience demonstrates true humility. Forgiveness and tolerance can then replace the sense of helplessness or victimization. Coupled with the understanding that everyone has made mistakes, and that it is honorable to correct such mistakes, the ability to surrender to limiting conditions also obliterates the notion of delusive perfection. In order to help it evolve past the existing limitations the soul puts the personality through a kind of "therapy." It should be remembered here that the soul is immortal and omnipresent. With or without the individual's conscious cooperation, it ultimately always coerces the power of evolution. The mortifying conditions persist even when karmic retribution cannot be accepted as such. It is necessary to persevere in the face of failure, and this in turn fosters development of steady willpower. Focused on fulfilling desires that lead to more equitable actions, the person learns to align with the natural laws of the universe.

Evolutionary necessity arises from violations against universal laws. Although the effects may be identical, the cause for failure or hardship is quite different. Rather than originating from wrong action, this present case of hardship is caused by avoidance of necessary life lessons. Instead of wrong action, it is non-action that is responsible for the limiting experiences. What was avoided in the past has reached a critical mass, and now the person is confronted with that which can no longer be avoided. Thus the necessity to face certain issues is inevitable. The soul has chosen circumstances that will finally enforce the evolutionary lessons shelved past their naturally tolerable time limit.

In the condition of karmic retribution, a static "hang in there" quality along with a need for self-effort fulfills the purpose of reflection, surrender, and determination. These qualities effect metamorphosis through self-knowledge and acceptance and will bring about the universal balance at some point. Even with the most humble stance of chagrin, grinding remorse, and cooperation with the circumstances, the individual is not in control to reach the point of requital. In the case of evolutionary necessity, on the other hand, the capacity to change is primarily in the person's hands. The individual is finally catching up on previously neglected areas of life. Acknowledging the underlying issues initiates a dynamic process. This knowledge makes it possible to realize the natural evolutionary intentions for individual's present life circumstances. Change often occurs rapidly once the necessary requirements are successfully met.

Determining whether the root cause of life events is karmic retribution or evolutionary necessity is complex. It is the intention of this book to lay the groundwork and supply some essential background information, which may spur an interest to ponder the issue. Wrong distinction between the two above described past life conditions may cause unnecessary damage. For example, someone who is experiencing the aftereffects of any type of childhood abuse or neglect may think that this is due to having been a violent or negligent parent in a past life him/herself. What if this is not at all the case? The person never even considered the possibility of evolutionary necessity. Perhaps this individual had many lifetimes where he or she avoided emotional issues. The result was a gross evolutionary imbalance. In order to continue on the path of soul progress it became necessary to experience the neglected areas at this point. Circumstances that were prominent enough to catch the person's attention brought this issue to the surface. Although not pleasant, the abuse event was effective enough to avoid further escape.

If this person were now thinking that she or he was an abuser in a past life, it would have severely adverse repercussions. It would appear as though the imposed circumstances were meant to force the individual to make amends for something that in fact never occurred. This information is not only wrong, it is harmful. Conversely, knowing that evolutionary necessity enforced the focus upon the area of emotional development enables much needed healing in that previously neglected sphere of life.

Another example for the possibility of wrong thinking in the context of karma and evolutionary necessity is the individual whose life is focused on external comfort and sensual enjoyment. Someone who loves affluence, beautiful environments, music, fine meals, and social gatherings for recreational purposes is not necessarily a person who avoids evolution and therefore accumulates bad karma by leading a "superficial" or indulgent lifestyle. This soul may have experienced grave hardship in previous lives, and now simply takes a break by fulfilling its desire for harmony, beauty, and prosperity. This is a viable way a soul can advance its development through the removal of earthly desires.

In a future incarnation this very soul may desire to contribute something extraordinary, and dedicate itself to a unique purpose. The individual may then experience some hardship due to circumstances resulting from this special task that requires sacrifices and focus on merely the essential aspects of existence. As a result there may be limited resources that force the person to live a simple, perhaps at times materially challenging life. Having experienced and enjoyed the comforts earthly living has to offer in a previous life, this soul will be able to fulfill its mission. Rather than being blocked by its own frustrated desires or destitute feelings of lack, it succeeds in persevering under adversity.

7. Cosmic Life Energy

Describing the step-down process of energy from the Source into the solid manifestation of matter is a difficult task. No material concept, model, or view can describe the interplay of spirit and matter accurately, and neither is language a suitable vehicle to convey this information. Nevertheless, an attempt at the impossible is made here. It is in the hope that rather than trapping the reader in the maze of rationalizations, the following will motivate contemplation and assimilation through the intuitive faculty of the mind. This way many insights occur of their own volition, and in their own time.

The Source is complete, undivided, ever-perfect, and all-encompassing oneness. As stated before, it nevertheless had a desire to turn its unity into diversity by creating the world of finite manifestations. The Source intended to keep a connection to all the parts of this manifested creation, so as not to dissolve into many shapes while losing harmony. Therefore, it created in such a way that its fundamental nature was contained within the entire creation of thought realm, spirit world of disembodied souls, as well as in the universe of inert matter with its various living entities.

Hence, the Source condensed its essence into cosmic life energy. The motion from unity into diversity, and the motion from diversity into unity became the two complementary forces of spirit and matter forever interacting with each other through the vehicle of cosmic life energy. Every atom contains as a primal building block this vital energy, which is less subtle than spirit but finer than matter. This medium of cosmic life energy ties the diversity of the countless manifested and subtle forms to wholeness with the one omnipresent Source.

This seamless fabric of life energy is the primal sound and light of the causal, and the astral realms. The vibratory thoughts of the Source manifest as ideas in the causal world, and the energetic vibration of light is the creative life energy of the astral world. Cosmic life energy reverberates at myriad frequencies also in the physical universe. The only difference between the mind and the body is the vibratory rate of the vital energy. Hence, there is no difference in substance between the two. Life energy can manifest as matter, emotion, thought, willpower, or at an even subtler level, as the ego. Various brain waves relate to different states of consciousness.

Just as we need solid food, liquids, air, and sunlight to support our body, so are various vibratory frequencies of cosmic life energy required to sustain us. It is not possible to open up the brain and find thought, or the ego, nor is it possible to find feelings in the heart or willpower in the stomach. Clearly, these human traits are there, but we do not have subtle enough instruments to measure the frequencies of their energetic vibration. Similarly, the primal light of the astral plane is not seen with the physical eyes, nor is the primal sound heard with the human ear. Their frequency is out of range for the physical sense organs. Viewing astral light is possible through the third eye of intuition only. Without this inner gaze of clairvoyant extrasensory perception the phenomenon of astral light remains unseen.

Some physicists postulate that light gives structure to matter, because they actually conceive of matter as frozen light. Oscillating light rays that move at a speed slower than light freeze into a matrix. The emerging pattern is mass, a condensed form of light. A seemingly paradox scientific discovery ties energy to matter in a similar way. Within the manifested universe every region in space is filled with various electromagnetic wave fields of different frequencies. Within such fields the minimum amount of energy a wave can possess is found in sectors of empty space. Although the waves in empty space hold the least amount of energy, one cubic centimeter of empty space contains more energy than all the matter in the universe!

A vast and measureless sea of energy is hidden at a subatomic level in empty space. Some scientists seem to have arrived at the same conclusion as saints, yogis, and other illuminated people: The greatest amount of energy is found beyond manifestation. Another scientific discovery further supports this fact. If we took out the empty space in each and every atom of the several trillion cells a human body comprises, we would then not be able to see this body any longer. Hence, the most important ingredient in matter is space, the seemingly empty, but in actuality by no means truly empty nothingness. In space we find the primal foundation, the ever-present and creative yet consistently intangible potential we call God.

Human beings sustain their life through the energy contained in solid, liquid, and gaseous substances. We take these substances into the body through food, liquids, and breathable air. In addition we need sunlight to keep the metabolic processes operative. Yet these substances are not the only sources of energy we draw into our bodies to maintain ourselves. Cosmic life energy is required as well. It is the real substance that keeps our heart beating, our intestines processing, and the consciousness adjusting from sleep to waking. Such energy is present in every atom and is what makes the electrons swirl around the nucleus. Even at a subatomic level the volition of cosmic life energy is what moves the basic building blocks of matter. These vital sparks of life energy maintain the body. We could look at this cosmic vital energy as the streamlined thoughts of the Source. Their vitalizing and rejuvenating subtle motion nurtures and sustains our physical, mental, and emotional being. From a metaphysical point of view, cosmic life energy is the building, ordering, preserving, coordinating, and restoring power of the body. Although cosmic energy does not hold the individual's consciousness, the soul does, this life energy permeates and sustains all levels of existence.

The flow of cosmic life energy between matter and consciousness must be free. Energy healing works directly with the subtle life force. Specific techniques often are used to target areas in the body that have become blocked. The blockage can be on any level. Working on the release of those obstructed subtle passageways will allow the cosmic life energy with its inherent intelligence to return to the area and heal the cells that are diseased. This can be done on a physical level with hands-on healing methods. If conscious or subconscious thoughts of failure, lack, limitation, or emotions such as fear or anger underlie the physical illness, however, they also have to be addressed. In order for permanent healing to occur, the person needs to become aware of negative habit patterns. They represent a source of impediment to the flow of life energy trying to reach the weakened areas. Spiritual afflictions also hinder the flow of the subtle life energy. Some examples are dogmatism; intellectual superiority; skepticism; lack of motivation, direction, or purpose; contentment with the material aspects of life; failure to recognize the natural principles that govern life; and ignorance of our invariable unity with the Source.

Just as energy healing is a way to tap into the flow of the intelligent life force, so can a positive attitude and conscious connection with the infinite power of the Source award a striving businessperson with success, or an aspiring artist with creativity. Even so, the moment this infinite power is taken for granted, that success or creative well may dry up. Healers can burn out and lose their healing touch. Rather than following the principles of prosperity in their trade, businesspeople might become attached to the wealth the organization is generating. They may then suddenly discover a mysterious decline of revenue. A writer too can experience writer's block; an actress may be struck by stage fright.

In the above examples the people are identifying with the cosmic energy by thinking that they are the starting point of their ingenuity. They perceive themselves as the sole power in charge of manifesting the desired results. Instead of realizing that the laws of prosperity and creativity are spiritual, and no one's personal possession, they forget themselves in the daze of their success. They begin to act from an egocentric place that operates antagonistically to the unifying intention underlying the manifestation of any truly successful activity.

Genuine success allows the life energy to flow freely through the vehicle of personal expression. Reflecting the unifying principle, it is based on actions that also include the happiness and welfare of others. Through self-maintenance strategies such as yoga or tai chi we can tap into the well of cosmic life energy and encourage its flow in our physical, mental and emotional body. Our existence is impermanent and changeable. The intelligent cosmic life energy is the connection between the finite experience of existence and the infinite nature of the soul. It echoes the immutable spiritual accord underlying all diversity.

8. Consciousness

In order to create the manifested universe, the Source divided itself into matter and consciousness. What once was subtle oneness began to exist in separate manifested forms with different states of conscious awareness. Consciousness exists in everything from a rock to a human being, and from a tree to a grasshopper. In itself formless, consciousness takes on the nature of various parts of creation. Once it is confined in a certain form, all experience is filtered through that specific limited consciousness. A cactus' consciousness is vastly different from that of a lion for example. Human consciousness is unique in that it possesses the evolutionary capability to expand. It can expand back to undivided oneness with the Source. Despite their separate human existence, enlightened people's consciousness is limitless. It is identified with the infinite cosmic consciousness of the Universal Source. This is a difficult concept for ordinary human comprehension, because our consciousness is conditioned by the experience of separation in a world of complementary opposites. We can supply a balance only through the application of right brain, inductive thinking.

On this planet there are five essential levels of consciousness. They are associated with the five basic life forms and the five elements. Each consecutive level has an additional capacity that makes consciousness more elaborate. A rock is confined to the inert matter state of consciousness associated with the earth element. It is crystallized, immobile, and therefore very dim and limited.

The next level is the quality of life energy affiliated with the fluid state of water. Plants need water to survive and fall into this category. Unlike rocks, whose life energy is frozen in solid mass, flowing life energy permeates plants. This is obvious in the growth and decay process they undergo. Although there is clearly a more distinct level of consciousness present, plants, just like rocks, do not possess an individual soul. Plants act as a species, and their evolution is regulated by the survival of the entire species or breed.

At the succeeding third level of consciousness, independent action discriminates the animal from the plants. Animals possess a nervous system and a brain with its sensor motor faculties and therefore have the ability to act in a self-governing way. According to the stimuli received from the environment through their senses, they behave independently from other members of the same species. The will that propels their actions is associated with the fire element. The driving force for their will is instinct. This level of consciousness additionally also allows for the presence of a soul. The soul qualities of one animal species could be compared with the soul of one individual human being. Therefore, evolution of the different animal species is still closely linked with all members of that particular species.

The human species represents the levels of consciousness associated with the elements of air and ether. Each person possesses an individual soul distinctly different and independent from all other souls. This is why evolution at the human level is highly individualized. The discriminating capability of the intellect is unique to human beings. Although all of creation is conscious, human beings are conscious of themselves, or conscious of being conscious. This special perception brings about the ability to reflect on and choose individual actions accordingly.

Other than using their intelligence for the purpose of survival, human beings also have the capacity to choose for more personal reasons. These reasons may be pleasure and entertainment, or they can also include more virtuous goals such as, for example, the interest to help others or to contribute in some major way to the evolution of the entire species. The caliber of a person includes feelings, sacrifice for the sake of others, and the potential for selfless love and compassion. These are functions associated with the air element.

Through the discriminating intellect it is possible to employ those latter qualities and act in ways that lead to an even higher degree of conscious awareness, which ultimately results in knowing the Universal Source. With expanded awareness the inherent laws of the cosmos progressively reveal themselves, and the individual naturally aligns behavior and actions accordingly. Instead of acting selfishly, people will be inclined to act in harmony with the universal laws of love and respect for all life. The choices become simpler, but it is more difficult to abide by those laws. It requires control of the senses, willpower, self-effort, concentration, discernment, and accurate analysis of one's behavior, motivations, or of any problem at hand.

Expanded awareness leads to an augmented desire to spiritualize, to consciously merge with the Source of all life. Through the discipline of applied intuitive insight and masterful detachment, the ability to discriminate brings more profound wisdom. At this advanced level people aspire to do the right thing regardless of personal gain. They know that when acting in harmony with universal principles, the gain is everlasting. This yielding action of the ego is the returning motion to unification with the Source. In order to successfully hold such perception it is necessary to stay detached. With this difficult step human souls can eventually complete their evolutionary journey and become spirit beyond the separation of matter and consciousness. The quality of absolute dispassion is associated with the element of ether, and as we know, is rarely attained. The element of ether gives rise to the four other elements. This explains why fully enlightened individuals can at will materialize or dematerialize their body, such as in the example of Jesus' resurrection after his crucifixion.

There are essentially three ways that promote conscious awareness. The first one is self-effort to vanquish the struggle of life. In Western societies people are conditioned to behave in codependent ways. Self-reliance and self-empowered initiative are often missing. This lack of autonomy can be seen in the phenomenon of the herd instinct, where the blind follow the blind. We also find it in the famous peer pressure that worries the parents of teenagers. Codependency operates in many personal connections, but especially is so also in intimate relationships. In certain areas contingent helplessness replaces self-sustaining efforts. Love songs tend to idealize codependency rather than mutual usefulness: "I love you, I need you, I cannot live without you." Many people in intimate relationships experience ordeals around addictions, abuse, and violence. The laws and customs of Western societies also support codependent behavior. This combination is why many spouses do not leave their abusive partner.

On a more collective level, television commercials and billboards advertise products to make life easier and seemingly more practical. Only, by now a million chores have been added to ensure that every moment is filled with essentially useless detail-oriented absurdity. Modern life has become tedious and complicated by gadgets that are supposed to be helpful. In almost every area of life the masses have been successfully trained in unnatural codependent behavior. People are frantically looking for something outside of themselves. They expect this outer thing to make life easier.

Isn't it time that we bring the conscious power back to the individual? When we rediscover our inherent sense of intuitive resourcefulness, we experience our own power. Thus we can then experience how our own efforts count. Satisfaction with the results of actions springing forth from self-effort automatically strengthens the sense of self-empowerment. This naturally replaces codependent behavior. What follows is the ability to have faith and trust in life, which in turn facilitates an expanded awareness of oneself in the world. None of this will take away the fact that life is a struggle, but it centers people in the awareness that it is their effort that matters, not necessarily the outcome. Hence, their unfolding consciousness is applied in practical, self-sustaining ways.

Making right choices is the second way that furthers the evolution of consciousness. Most people's choices are limited by past conditioning. They choose largely due to habit and a sense of trepidation or restrained potentialities. Their material reality is filled with obligations. There seems to be no time to focus on personal development and physical and emotional welfare, not to mention the practice of some spiritual discipline. Yet no real growth can occur if the subtler realms of psychological and spiritual existence are neglected or repressed. Right choices involve taking all aspects of existence into consideration.

Some choices go against acquired subconscious habit patterns, and can therefore seem foreign or even wrong. If we make beneficial choices, then these choices are in fact right, even if it does not feel right at first. To understand and recognize this to be true is often just what enables us to do the right thing. As we summon the courage to make the right choice and act accordingly, we transform our limitations. As we do, our consciousness naturally evolves toward expanded awareness. This also refers back to the chapter on evolution. It is an example for how gradual change is more likely to occur with our cooperation. If on the other hand we do not check our inherent resistance to change, it can bring on cataclysmic events.

The third route that promotes conscious awareness is meditation or a similar method of one-pointed concentration on the Source. All of creation is conscious and interrelated through subatomic particles. These subatomic particles comprise cosmic energy. While resonating at a unifying frequency the entire manifested universe is connected through this energetic level. Cosmic life energy is the link between consciousness and matter. If we can control this energy, we can control our consciousness. In order to comprehend this interrelatedness, human beings can employ a practical system such as meditation. Thus it is possible to realize the unity of the entire creation through direct perception. The desire to experience this universal connectedness is the transcending impulse and stimulates development of conscious awareness.

The transcending impulse activated by meditation or any other authentic spiritual discipline becomes a felt sense, an actual experienced reality. This process takes place through a gradual shift from identifying oneself with the body and ego to the soul. We can gain the insight that our soul's being indeed is infinite. Beyond the confines of the body, life and death become merely different states of consciousness. The path of meditation leads humans from the experience of being individuals with a finite rational understanding to comprehending themselves as intuitive souls. The body at some point will cease to exist, but the essence is infinite and forever linked with the Source. From this vastly different viewpoint we realize that our ordinary earthly experience of separateness in the final analysis is an illusion.

Once life and death are seen as different states of consciousness, the emotional attachment to either one of these states is diminished. It is much easier to act harmoniously with the laws of nature if one is not intimidated by the boundaries of the finite reality. Instead of being at the mercy of worldly events that continuously threaten one's survival in one form or another, it then becomes possible to view life from an infinite place of connectedness to Spirit. From this bond emanates love for all life. It is a conscious love that creates true happiness, the famous state of bliss. Bliss originates from the realization that the soul is forever linked with the Source, whose essence is unconditional love. From such a vantage point we only want to do good and act on the principles of love and kindness. Through this frequency we can tune into the lasting happiness of the soul.

Even when meditating regularly, this expanded state of consciousness is not easily accessible. It is a condition that may be experienced for a few moments on occasion. In the beginning the efforts toward achieving a deep meditative state often are unsatisfactory, and if judged as such in the moment may look discouraging. It is important to follow a scientific method of practice where the focus is kept with the object of meditation such as a mantra or the breath. Since the effects are cumulative, the continuous effort will gradually lead to deeper concentration. With steady meditation practice the number of such connected moments in our conscious awareness increases. It is as though the individual was having a love affair with the Creator. Every moment we are able to spend connecting through one-pointed concentration with our own soul and with the Source is a moment spent in bliss and inner happiness. This is accompanied by deeper intuitive insights that lead to different choices and various changes in our outward reality. Our experience may begin to inspire other people. We might develop a calling to be a teacher and pass on a specific form of meditation or a spiritual system. Over many lifetimes it becomes possible to continuously maintain one's conscious center of gravity in the above-described expanded state of awareness. As mentioned earlier, this leads to the final liberation of the soul from the earthly plane of existence.

A spiritual method without self-effort and right choice making will not develop our consciousness in an all-encompassing way. It is necessary to follow these three routes simultaneously. Only then will the evolution of conscious awareness produce the results of inner happiness and gradual self-realization. For example, giving more importance to the spiritual aspect than to the emotional and the material aspects of existence can produce a one-sided consciousness lacking in actual life experience. Likewise, if all available time were invested solely in right choice making leading to actions in the world, the psychological and spiritual components would be lacking.

The natural law of cause and effect, the laws of evolution, as well as all other natural laws are exacting and self-effecting. When a person's approach in life is balanced relative to worldly, physical, emotional, mental, and spiritual awareness, consciousness increases in a comprehensive manner. Although development may be slower at first, in the long run it is nevertheless a lot more steadfast than one-sided advancement in one of these areas. Since all realms of existence are developed without any significant setbacks resulting in delays, this is also less frustrating. Remembering this is beneficial when we seek to understand and cooperate with our evolutionary development.

For a certain amount of time it is possible to focus more on a particular aspect of human existence. Therefore, our awareness develops accordingly. At a certain point, however, no further growth can occur. In order to continue the evolutionary journey we need to employ a more balanced approach. If we avoid this, then we are about to skip steps. Without first taking care of the neglected areas of life, these skipped steps will result in circumstances that make further growth impossible. This leads to the previously covered condition of evolutionary necessity. Evolutionary necessity then will take precedence over other issues, which can be an extremely frustrating experience. While we are forced to deal with the same issue over and over, other activities and aspects of life have been relegated to the sidelines. Of course, this is only the narrow perspective of the ego that perceives things in this limited way.

Here it becomes obvious how knowledge of the soul can be of great assistance by helping us view our life in a much more comprehensive way. Although we would never consciously choose such an unpleasant treadmill, we are able to realize that this is inevitable for soul growth. The soul subconsciously knows what is necessary. Once we understand that the circumstances enforced against our will are in the foreground because they previously have been avoided, we gain the ability to cooperate and bring them to completion. In order to work them through, these issues need to be developed consistently. They will continue to emerge until the entire issue is fully integrated. This is how we recover the skipped steps and grow toward a balanced conscious awareness.

Furthermore, different facets of our consciousness naturally develop at different rates. Cataclysmic events only take place when one area becomes blocked because of resistance or over-identification. As long as development continues within each facet, evolution proceeds in a gradual fashion. Regardless, some areas of life may be more developed. At the same time we can feel that in other spheres of our existence we are nowhere near as accomplished. This may result in a lack of confidence in those areas. The moment we concentrate and make an effort toward developing them, these less proficient realms of existence begin to pick up. Just like the butterfly emerging from the chrysalis needs to struggle to gain the strength to fly once it frees itself, this effort is necessary to keep the evolutionary balance.

9. Complementary Opposites

We experience life through polarities of complementary opposites such as hot and cold, day and night, greed and generosity, good and evil, growth and decay. All of creation is set up to function in this field of dualistic tension within time and space reality. Human language is based on the agreement to label dynamics, objects, and living things with specific names. We derive meaning and perspective through comparison. All phenomena, objects, and living entities are measured and compared in relation to one another. Without contrasting opposites we would not know how to describe or classify a single thing, nor could we express any outer or inner experience. Day becomes meaningful against the backdrop of night, and we can name sadness because we know joy.

There are two major forces in the manifested universe. The first one is the unifying principle that brings all of creation back to the Source. This force is love, the divine attraction in creation that harmonizes, binds together, and consolidates everything. Its polarity is repulsion, the outgoing cosmic energy that separates and discriminates. This energy projected out from the Source is what materializes creation. In essence it is the delusion of separateness that the Hindu ideology calls "Maya." Within the boundaries of time and space, however, matter indeed is finite, and any object or living entity is separate from everything else around it. As human beings these are margins we cannot extend beyond. The means to gain conscious experience away from dualistic reality is to complement our rational mind with the intuitive knowing of our soul. In this realm we find healing from division. This is a state experienced in trance or spiritual ecstasy.

In coping with the tension of the complementary poles, human beings have the opportunity to choose between the extremes. Of course, most of the time things are not so clearcut in either direction. All along the journey of earthly existence shades of gray obscure the polarities. We gauge our way striving to choose balance in our actions and in our being. Because life plays out mostly within the moderate scope of shades of gray, it takes much time and experience to see the extremes hidden within this appearance.

When we do, we are still often misled by a smokescreen, which hinders us to clearly see the polarity. We may go along with a process or a condition thinking that it is leading us in the intended direction, only to find out at some point along the road that in fact it is not. Trial and error helps us gain the experience necessary to choose a better path next time. Still, life is so complex and changeable that often we are left with more trial and error activity. Even as we grow with experience, there is still plenty of room for uncertainty and miscalculation. Whatever decision we make may be neither all right nor all wrong. This too is due to the dualism within our universe. Time will tell whether a decision was right. Additionally, our perspective might change again at a later point. This can allow a different perception of the situation, and may help us to change course along the way.

Just like evolution and karma, relativity is a natural directive. The ability to stay adaptable and flexible is of great importance. The human organism managed to evolve as far as it did thanks to its capacity to adapt to change. Within this lies a great power of survival. There is no inherent state of ultimate perfection that could save us from making these moment-to-moment choices. The only perfection is the strength to choose well from one moment to the next. Hidden behind the shades of gray that obscure the polarities there is a roadmap. The inner voice of our human conscience is also a natural directive.

Conscience always indicates the right and wrong actions and thoughts within the scope of attraction and repulsion. It points to unity and inclusion instead of diversity and separation. Our conscience intuitively knows the truth about the motivations behind our actions. Discriminating between considerate, kind, and scrupulous causes, as opposed to selfish, greedy or corrupt motives, our ethical sense lets us know where we are really coming from. Whether we are inclined to listen to this intuitive knowledge available to us is a matter of choice. Given the effort to cooperate with the attraction pole within the dualistic universe, our awareness teamed with increasing wisdom and determination becomes stronger and more skilled at knowing when our conscience is not clear. We can grow proficient at guiding our actions by consistently aligning them with the intuitive truth of our conscience. Acting with sincerity in respect to our intentions is a way to gain inner harmony. By extension this also is beneficial to other people.

Attraction toward unity and repulsion into diversity correlates with the two antagonistic desires of the soul. As we have seen in the chapter on desire, these are on the one hand all the earthly longings, and on the other hand the desire to reunite with the Source. Every time we base our choice on wholeness and inclusion relative to benefiting self and others, we indirectly choose the principle of attraction. This is the harmonizing principle of love and devotion. The direction of the energy is pointing toward the Source. When we choose one of our own earthly desires, our action is in alignment with the antagonistic pole of repulsion. This is the separating force. It correlates with energy moving away from the Source. This propensity intends to keep things in the finite form of manifested reality. This conflicting and diversifying impulse leads to more complexity and new desires and attachments. It is this bondage to things, to our body, to emotions, to fixed beliefs or thought patterns, as well as to our values that reinforces an egocentric stance. This tends to keep us separate from the sense of belonging to something more powerful and omnipresent than our constant struggle to succeed as a separate entity in a world full of antagonism, contradiction, complexity, and confusion.

Within our mind the dualistic nature of earthly existence is embodied in the two hemispheres of the cerebral cortex. The nonlinear, inductive thinking of the right brain that works with pictures, inclinations, symbols, and premonitions signifies inclusive oneness. The relativity of matter-bound existence is represented in the rational, deductive, logical reasoning of the left brain. The linear thoughts signify the motion of cosmic energy projected away from the Source. They are the thoughts of complexity, diversity, analysis, logic, and practicality. In regard to cosmological comprehension, using the thinking of this hemisphere is quite ineffective. Seeing the whole picture of what it means to be a living human being on this planet is not a rational function. With linear thinking there is no definite conclusion on how to put the fragments of these thoughts together into undivided wholeness. Rather, it is like a revolving door of continuous perspectives that keeps coming up with new ways of seeing the issue at hand, without ever arriving at a truly satisfying conclusion. Thus, the intellect views everything by being apart from it. In order to satisfy the rational thought process, the intellect continually creates more separate and finite images that are compulsively connected in logical or analytical ways.

The right hemisphere of the nonlinear, symbolic, and intuitive thinking on the other hand is tuned in to the energy that binds together and adapts the view toward wholeness. Oneness is beyond what we can comprehend rationally in the finite earthly existence of phenomenal reality. Within right brain oriented activities, such as intuitive contemplation, music, or dance, as well as all ritualistic or trance states, the limitations of the mind are metamorphosed into unity. The cosmological and universal meaning of existence becomes a felt sense and an actual experience.

Good is the manifestation of love and inclusion, the true nature of the Source. Evil is the delusional force of separation leading to stagnation, disease, and eventually to destruction. In human life the battlefield of these two forces is played out through our earthly desires in the arena of the ego and the soul. Attachment to satisfying these desires creates fear and anger. Fear is invoked by the thought of not being able to have these desires and needs met. Anger is the emotional response if the fulfillment of the desires is obstructed. Through temptation and the promise of worldly pleasures the cosmic force of delusion tends to turn the individual away from right action and his or her own conscience.

There is no evolution within a consciousness oriented exclusively toward egotism and materialism. As long as this attitude prevails, actions based on these selfish goals perpetuate the status quo. Many traditional religious customs also have lost their connection with eternal truths in favor of dogma and hypocritical interests such as popularity, comfort, or greed. All too often these customs have been reduced to perfunctory routines that no longer reflect the laws of life. Empty conventions cannot serve or guide people in appropriate ways. This has become a real predicament because many human beings need some direction in the cosmological comprehension of their lives. The sense of being lost in a dualistic world, not knowing what to think or believe, keeps people in a state of bewilderment during times when true guidance is critical. Wise counsel with regard to the right choices in the struggle and quandaries of existence is a truly necessary function.

Individuals who are willing and eager to grow and evolve actualize their intuitive capacity with the help of devotion and willpower. While adhering to guiding spiritual principles they develop their conscience around the desire to act in accordance with the natural laws of the universe. Everything required in the evolutionary process is naturally provided by the Source in the interplay of spirit and matter. Letting go of excessive control and finite concepts allows for limitations to be transmuted. When trusting that the next step appears at the right time, we realize that the interconnectedness of matter and spirit is a dynamic that never fails.

All along the way the delusion of separateness is eagerly awaiting every possible opportunity to tempt, conflict, and deceive us from reaching our worthwhile goals. This force will do so in ever more subtle ways, changing course with each turn we take. With every adjustment we make, evil that creates the delusion of limited resources and lack of power evolves along with our growing awareness. Encouraging the stance of separateness and egocentric attachment, it changes its game just enough to keep below the conscious threshold. Before we catch onto this game, the next snag obstructs the road. Already more energy to halt and reflect is needed. This requires analysis with crystal clear detachment, objective observation and correlation, and finally courage to start anew.

To persevere in the face of evil's silent opposition, cunning deception, and compelling temptation is a necessary test of strength. The struggle between the antagonistic poles of attraction signifying awakening in spirit and repulsion representing entrapment in matter grows ever more treacherous and fierce. Determination on this path becomes even more important. When we use logic along with heartfelt compassion we are following the natural dynamic from decline into darkness of materialism to ascension back into the spiritual light of wisdom. The soul's evolutionary journey leads along this path. For most of us it is not a conscious experience. Nevertheless, when we cooperate with our soul's intentions we are more likely to experience a smooth journey. This cooperation is represented by the desire to do good, to include others in our considerations, and to share. Egocentric resistance signified by greed, hunger for power, and selfish exclusion of others augments evil's bondage to the finite world of matter. The evolutionary force within our soul will sooner or later break it. This experience is cataclysmic.

The dualistic interplay of matter and Spirit through involution and evolution is described in a biblical myth. Lucifer once was an archangel of God. In his divine mission he had the freedom to create independently. His sovereignty was a token of achievement from his Creator. Lucifer was an obedient and humble servant of his master. He was involved in spreading the message of virtue, purity, kind behavior, and right action. While acting as a mentor and a bearer of light, he compassionately guided simpler beings.

After a perfected mundane existence Goddess called all beings to come back from their manifested existence in the world of relativity. At that time the entire manifested creation had reached a point of saturation. Lucifer too was instructed to return to the Great Spirit. He had grown so attached to his abilities to create autonomously, however, that he refused to obey his Creator. God wanted all souls to return of their own free will. The love of the Great Spirit for its creation was so immense that Lucifer was not forced to return. This one being's disobedience had a tremendous consequence: the manifested creation could not be dissolved, and all creatures had to stay in their materialized form. Lucifer's defiance provoked one great repercussion. His choice resulted in being cast out of heaven, that place where spirit ideas are manifested and dissolved by sheer thought. He no longer was able to act as a bearer of light.

Lucifer assured his desire to stay separate by keeping human beings from evolving toward the light. He knew they would seek to know the Source. Once humans evolved in this way, there would no longer be a need for a materialistic universe. So Lucifer began to secretly influence mortals by steering them away from devotional love and reverence for their Creator. He became evil. He decided to trick, mislead, tempt, confuse, deceive, seduce, and compel human beings to follow his ill will. In this array of covert games Lucifer recruited them into his army to fight the battle against God, whom he now passionately hated. From that moment on, all who listened to him fell prey to the bondage to limiting matter bound circumstances. This identification generated one delusion after the other.

Although gratification through attachment to the apparent reality of our external existence can never bring lasting happiness, this compelling force began to beguile human beings in the areas where they were the weakest. The consequence of Goddess' decision to let Lucifer have his own way was that the rest of the manifested universe became subject to bondage, which lead to misery, pain, and suffering. In order to liberate from this, everyone now has to work hard to overcome the influence of Lucifer's evil game. For those individuals who are able to discriminate right from wrong, good from evil, ego bondage from soul freedom, Lucifer once again turns into the bearer of light. For them he shines the light of conscious awareness onto the darkness of illusion.

This creation myth depicts the complementary forces in the relativity of manifested existence. All humans experience this dualism through the previously described dual desires in the soul. These are all the sense- and matter-bound desires, and on the other hand the desire to return to the Source. In the myth the gravitational pull of the senses, and the strong need for material satisfaction through ego consciousness is personified in this fallen angel of God. The myth shows that soul freedom is achieved through ascension from matter into spirit. Unless a person is able to let go and transcend his or her ego consciousness into the limitless God consciousness, there is no escape from the endless treadmill of desires. Many roads lead to the same place, and a diversity of means of traveling can be utilized to get there. Sooner or later anyone who chooses such a path along with a vehicle of transportation, will arrive at that very same destination. Likewise, there is a great variety of spiritualizing methods that all produce the same result.

Lucifer's story also shows an important point in how the Source is not perfect in its manifested aspect. In other words, the concept of perfection within worldly existence is an illusion. The only way to know perfection is by surrendering the rational mind into the vast realm of intuitive inner knowing. Through the step-by-step process of transforming limitations, evolution toward an ever-increasing depth of spiritual realizations can occur. With the gradual ascension of matter into spirit the finite experience of existence is metamorphosed. Perfection exists exclusively in the world of spirit, of which the soul is a part. The mystery of existence stays veiled until an individual by sheer desire, deep devotion, and single-minded focus reaches liberation of his or her consciousness.

The most important point in the creation myth of Lucifer is the aspect of the bearer of light. Through reversing the flow of energy from matter to spirit, wisdom transcends temptation and confusion. When we seek the truth regardless of what we are compelled to choose by habit, greed, lack of discrimination, or weakness, then the bearer of light becomes the guide to right action. Wisdom bestows clarity to see the outcome of a choice before making it, and thus aids in finding the courage and the willpower to choose in new and empowering ways.

In essence, God is the origin of everything, and that includes the darkness of evil. Again, in the manifested universe perfection only exists as an abstract idea. In actual reality there is no such thing, only a striving to become better one step at the time. We need to keep this point in mind when progress is slow, or when we seem to revert back to old ways. It is also a helpful reminder when we do not see our spouses, children, parents, coworkers, or our friends, change their less than desirable ways. Even if there has not been any light for thousands of years, the darkness in a cave is banished immediately by the flashlight of an explorer who enters it. Never mind how long darkness existed or how many times we have made the same mistake, when we see a way out we can change in that very moment. This is the bearer of light in action. Change occurs in the moment we decide to think and act differently. This also inspires us to see the effort as more important than the outcome.

PART TWO

WORLD CYCLES

10. Life's Natural Principles

Life's natural directives are intrinsic to the manifested universe; they are timeless truths that never change. Scientists have discovered some of them, such as, for example, the law of gravity, the fact that the Earth rotates around the Sun, and that bacteria are killed when exposed to hot temperatures. Natural principles are inherent to human behavior as well. Much of what we call common sense is based on natural directives. For example, no one in her or his right mind would leave a 2-year-old child without direct supervision, nor would anyone go for a walk barefoot when it is minus ten degrees outside. We possess an inherent sense of right and wrong that guides us in our actions, reflection, and planning.

Customs, laws, rules, and regulations are essential in all societies. People live together and depend on one another for mutual usefulness and survival. The laws they create may or may not be congruous with life's natural directives. When they are not, then human beings are living against their inherent purpose and intentions. Instead of allowing all aspects of their lives to exist as equally relevant and valuable, those that are against the norm and set rules of that specific society need to be suppressed. People can no longer express themselves according to their true nature. Consequently their psychology and behavior become altered in dysfunctional ways.

The ensuing warped effects of suppression also result in a social structure that tolerates exploitative behavior. This is especially puzzling in societies that are built on democracy, the law of equality and justice for all citizens. The hypocrisy obvious in this contradiction leads back to the suppression of life's natural aspects. In modern societies actions related to the intellect are considered more important and valuable than actions associated with the body and the emotions. How could there possibly be any truth in a feeling being less valid than a thought? All realms of our human existence are of course equally important. The crucial point is how we relate to and act within any and all of these realms. Are our intentions pure, devious, and so on, and how do we conduct ourselves with regard to those intentions? This is where value judgments are appropriate.

Through intellectual leverage human beings tend to see themselves as separate from and superior to the rest of creation. Owing to this unreal stance, people create standard behaviors, moral codes, taboos, and regulations that do not fit the category of natural principles. In essence, they begin to think that the universe is there to serve them. Therefore, they are then entitled to take as much as they please without consideration for the total balance of life.

When greed and hunger for power becomes the prime directive, humans tend to take advantage of others. Some use the Darwinist "survival of the fittest" theory for justification. In fact nothing other than self-interest and ruthless acquisitiveness is hidden behind this conveniently rational approach. By example it sets a standard of conduct for others in similar situations to follow suit. In conjunction with such cultures belief systems were invented to subjugate and control the weaker, less aggressive people. With this transition the modern structure of a few that hold the wealth of all was established. It is based on distortion created through unnatural tenets.

In a social order that is aligned with life's natural directives there is no need for such measures. Societies built on a foundation of such directives include the entire creation as equally relevant and sacred. Emotional involvement and intuitive truths of equality, compassion, sharing, and inclusion are vital to human existence. Indeed, the integrity of any society depends upon such values. Every state of consciousness and every work position within a system is necessary and vital for the functioning of the whole. What role any given member plays within society depends on many factors such as talent, family background, karma, and personal interests. Value judgments based on these choices are a shortsighted and tragic mistake. They do not honor the integrity of the system. Such concepts are foreign to societies whose members act, feel, and reason in alignment with life's natural truths. This is illustrated with the example of indigenous cultures, where all roles within society are respected equally. Therefore, all members are the same in status as well. Such models of social order allow for balance, mutual respect, justice, and shared responsibility in the welfare of all.

Even though they were not knowledgeable in the ways of modern cultures, the preceding indigenous cultures were much closer to the intrinsic laws of nature. Modern cultures are based on rationally practical principles. Pragmatic knowledge created a chain reaction where deductive thinking eventually crowded out intuition along with a feeling of wholeness. This caused disrespect for nature and was also lacking in regard for human life. Although individuation equaled progress, the specific ways in which this occurred resulted in loss of important life aspects, which also contributed to social alienation. After abandoning the inherent impulses, their replacement with laws that were motivated by greed and exploitation caused fragmentation and trauma.

Of course modern existence cannot return to the ways of life and belief systems ancient cultures held. Yet it is necessary to recover the suppressed aspects that cause dissonance. Although rational thinking has brought much progress, it lacks concepts based on respecting all of nature and all peoples as equally valid and beneficial to life on Earth. When these principles are embraced once more, the process of reintegrating a felt sense of wholeness can occur. Individuation in tandem with collectively cultivating the pertinent component of intuition will move evolution past trauma and fragmentation. Through realigning with life's natural directives we can balance rational concepts with intuitive truth.

The question becomes how to strengthen the individualized benefits of our modern era while reintegrating views that foster social cohesiveness. How can we learn from past and present conditions to move toward a synergy of technology with natural directives? And how can we eliminate the negative byproducts so that life on this planet may continue in harmony with its intended purpose? To find some answers we are going to explore the vast and very distinct cycles of becoming that we are part of here on Earth.

11. The Great Galactic Cycle

As previously stated, in the time and space based universe of relativity everything manifests through complementary polarities such as hot and cold, night and day, and attraction and repulsion. This phenomenon also is present in human consciousness. Oscillation between diametrically opposed points facilitates awareness. These polarities give human beings the perspective of cognitively grasping the basic concepts of existence.

Without contrasts we would be lost in a sea of indistinguishable sensations. We could not compare an event to previous occurrences. How would we know right, if we had not experienced wrong? We would not be able to differentiate nor could we arrive at the right conclusion. The contrast between complementing poles allows us to make a distinction, which leads us in a specific direction. In the world of relativity comparison and making clear decisions is dependent on deductive thinking.

Nonetheless, this type of thinking is limited by nature. In order to see the bigger picture, we need to integrate the logical conclusions with insight. If applied without intuitive balance, deductive thinking can lead to false reasoning.

Matter and consciousness are two complementary states of one origin: spirit. Consciousness in human form can know about matter and spirit. When identified with matter, it is ego consciousness. When identified with spirit, it is soul consciousness. As discussed in the first part of this book, the purpose of our evolutionary journey is to progress from ego to soul consciousness. In this way we eventually achieve mastery of the physical plane. At that point we rise above the world of relativity, and our individual consciousness becomes omniscient. Until this can be a personal reality, our consciousness is subject to the forces of polarization in the finite reality of time and space.

Evolution is contrasted by involution, in view of the fact that this pair of opposites too is part of the tension set up in the field of relativity. Involution is the contracting, solidifying, and individuating motion from spirit to matter, and evolution the expanding, unfolding progression that metamorphoses the limitations from the finite matter bound state back to spirit. These complementary polarities sequencing expansion and contraction are reflected in a special cycle we are part of here on Earth. It is called the Great Galactic Cycle. This little-known galactic occurrence is what we will use to measure the times relative to the phenomena of our modern era.

Picture the Great Galactic Cycle as an indefinitely alternating sequence of expansion equaling light and contraction equaling darkness. Moreover, the phase of light represents the refined consciousness of evolution, and the phase of darkness the limited materialistic perception of involution. The nature of the Great Galactic Cycle is subtle and has not yet been identified by any contemporary scientific method. Be that as it may, Eastern saints and sages have passed on the knowledge of the subtle laws that govern manifest existence. They have always been aware of this cyclic metaphysical dynamic. It consists of an implied motion by which the sun rotates around a fixed star. In this trajectory the sun approaches and draws back from a Grand Center. On the physical plane this Grand Center corresponds to the center of the Milky Way galaxy.

From a more comprehensive viewpoint the Grand Center is the seat of creative power comprised of subtle electromagnetic vibrations. Here life is tuned to the specifications that enable the workings of the manifested creation in this galaxy to proceed. It is really their blueprint, which emits the energetic guidance for all natural directives. The Grand Center acts as a subtle relay station for the ultimate power and supreme intelligence that governs all of life. The relay station shifts the amount of cosmic energy from higher to lower vibrations. The step-down process adjusts and relates these frequencies to the different levels of existence. Thought, for example, has a higher vibratory rate than the physical body. If any specific vibration is not tuned exactly to its fundamental nature, it cannot exist as it is meant to be.

The location where the sun is closest to the Grand Center coincides with the time of sophisticated spiritual knowledge. Human beings are in harmony and direct experience of life's natural directives. They possess mental control over their physical being. The body is governed by the mind so that any defective body part can be healed, even in case of serious damage. People also have a keen sense of the subtler levels of existence, namely, the astral and causal planes. It is a time when most of them conceive the abstractions of the interplay between matter and spirit without any difficulties. These concepts are simply inherent to their lucid perception. Differences in consciousness between people still exist during the expanded light phase of the cycle, but because it is easier to advance in the metaphysical realms of life, a higher ratio of people progresses spiritually. This does not mean that their awareness reaches omniscience.

The Great Galactic Cycle

The point where the sun is farthest from the Grand Center equals darkness. The human mind becomes so dull and impenetrable that most people can no longer grasp anything beyond the gross material level. It also expresses itself in wrong thinking and lack of mental power. The mind/body connection is lost, and the mind has forgotten how to govern and direct the physical cells to heal and maintain optimum health throughout a full lifespan. Disease becomes acceptable as an unavoidable byproduct of living. It is much feared and fought in more or less ineffective ways. People are the prisoners of their own physical structure. In the density of materialism the body rules the mind that has forgotten it has all the power necessary to command the physical cells to operate in harmony. During this phase of the Great Galactic Cycle approximately eighty percent of all mind activity is not consciously known. During the light phase this percentage is much smaller, which is connected with the powerful sovereignty of the conscious mind over matter.

By the calculations of the galactic astrologer Swami Sri Yukteswar (1855 - 1936) the Great Galactic Cycle was recognized as being of equal length to the cycle of the zodiac. This cycle is approximately 26,000 years and will be discussed in the next chapter. Before Sri Yukteswar made the adjustment, the cycle of expansion and contraction in human consciousness ascribed the contractive pole of darkness an oppressive length of more than 400,000 years! Sri Yukteswar's adjustment allowed for a liberating viewpoint of the developmental dynamics involved in human consciousness. It did so for two reasons.

First, the relatively short cycle is a relief in and of itself. The perspective of 400,000 years of darkness shrouding human cognizance is depressing even for the most optimistic at heart. Second, because it was paralleled with the cycle of the zodiac, Sri Yukteswar's cycle provides a way to grasp time in synchrony with archetypal, astrological, and historical sequences. Accordingly, we can put the trials of the present era into perspective. Although it does not necessarily guarantee smooth and gradual development, the ensuing solutions are still reassuring.

Involution and evolution of the Great Galactic Cycle's descending and ascending arcs provide the necessary stimulation for human consciousness in the experience of relativity. The seed to know the Source that represents the principle of love, union, and the desire to act with pure intentions is planted in the Great Galactic Cycle's light phase. Then progressive separation from this awareness gives each individual a moment-to-moment choice. It is the individual's navigational journey through the maze of shades of gray. People struggle to keep in touch with happiness and truth. Although it is difficult, this struggle promotes growth. If there were only a time for all humans to be in total harmony with the Source, stagnation would soon be reached. Everyone would be happy in a state where natural directives and lucid perception govern all areas of life. Due to lack of incentive from the relativity of existence, very few would make an individual effort to further evolve. This complacent state counteracts the ultimate purpose, which is to reach enlightenment through individual effort.

During the dark phase of the Great Galactic Cycle the lack of the mind's sovereignty over matter is also evident in the realm of feelings and emotions. Because they are disconnected from the truth of their own intentions and desires, it is hard for people to distinguish their motives. They are inclined to blindly follow what feels good on the spot. This is linked with a deep inner emptiness, which makes it difficult to know who they are and what to value beyond the tangible or the imagined. Compensation through fantasy, addiction, compulsion, or hedonistic living runs rampant.

Because this phase of the cycle is farthest from the Grand Center, the laws people create go out of sync with natural directives. Human beings tend to fall prey to the evils that accompany attachment to matter. To name but a few, such negative attributes are greed, egotism, hunger for power, aversion, pride, self-righteousness, vengeance, prejudice, ignorance, and hypocrisy. The defiant stance of separateness augments contention, strife, and war. The way human beings treat one another and their environment feeds off desires for ego gratification at the expense of love, respect for all life, and what is actually true. The bondage to material values perverts clarity, integrity, and the desire for union. It is easy for an oblivious collective consciousness to be influenced and then exclusively guided by material thoughts. The induced greed results in degenerate actions and corruption.

During the dark phase of the cycle this temptation to stay ensnared in a consciousness that corroborates material existence creates a powerful illusion of separateness. Even so, the sense of separateness also promotes the dynamic to individuate. When the separating desires have been exhausted, individual consciousness tends to turn to the fact that there must be more to existence than what meets the eye. This in sequence leads to the conscious individual desire to know the Source. With this newly defined purpose the ambition to reach the goal through self-effort and determination gradually follows. Hence, the dark phase of the Great Galactic Cycle is just as necessary for the soul's evolutionary journey as the light phase of subtle perception.

In every cycle the process of involution leading to evolution happens differently. Each cycle has its own specific way in which dullness takes hold in the consciousness of human beings. Human egos are deceived in new ways, and the collective consequences occur accordingly. Because of the time frame being so very large we have little to no insight into how exactly this occurred in the previous cycles. However, the dynamic is universal. Limitations in consciousness occur progressively during involution in the descending arc of the cycle. Through their metamorphosis in the expansive phase, the previously acquired or imposed limitations benefit evolution. During the ascending arc this metamorphosis ensures the development of human awareness in new ways. Through the collective unconscious all human beings remember this along with the information of previous evolutionary cycles.

The subconscious mind of each person additionally holds explicit developments concerning past lives. This information depends on any given soul's individual journey from lifetime to lifetime. How much information is relevant or directly accessible depends on the specific lessons, and on the evolutionary state itself. Past this dark peak of the Great Galactic Cycle human laws are out of sync relative to natural directives. People suffer from the distorted effects this created within their own psyche. In this time the need for healing becomes maximized. It also often is necessary to work out unresolved past life issues. When past life events are unsettled, they continue to disturb the individual's ability to fully function in the present. The capacity to remember and relive in order to resolve becomes vital. At the present time religious conditioning does not allow for a perspective that includes past life recollection as a reality. Therefore, the majority of people are not yet receptive to this perspective.

The beginning of the Great Galactic Cycle's expansive motion coincides with souls being born who desire to work out issues they acquired during the dark phase of the cycle. It can express itself in skipped steps, where the soul has been trying to rush ahead, while neglecting important areas of its evolution. This reinforces the phenomenon of evolutionary necessity as discussed in one of the earlier chapters. It also can manifest in traumas from the past or past lives and the need for healing of such traumas. Whatever dynamics are no longer helpful for developmental continuation need to be purged from the consciousness. Unresolved trauma is one of the phenomena that let us know there is work to do in this area.

Now we are faced with a greater than ever array of dysfunctions that interfere with people's normal behavior, competent action, ability to cope with ordinary life stress, and their basic need for wholeness and well-being. Healing can occur only if we deal with the wounds. These manifestations are a necessity for the individual as well as collective evolution of the human species. The above dynamics of involution and evolution pertaining to the

Great Galactic Cycle offer a fundamental background. Understanding the origin of the wounds of modern living in this light allows for a holistic view that no current system can offer. Our understanding of what was, what is, and what is likely to come will expand greatly after looking at the historical events described in the following chapters.

12. The Cycle of the Zodiac

From an astrological standpoint the zodiac is a belt of star constellations positioned around the ecliptic. These constellations form the backdrop for the phenomena of planetary movements we observe from Earth. Each star constellation of the zodiac is associated with an astrological sign. The signs symbolize specific archetypes of human experience. These are functions and qualities of life relevant for all people.

The astrological cycle of the zodiac is also linked with time-specific phenomena, and as such is quite useful in describing chronological epochs in human history. In this capacity the cycle is a reflection of the wobble of the Earth's axis. What observation and correlation has shown regarding this terrestrial motion is most interesting to consider. Every time the Earth's axis points toward the border of the previous constellation of the zodiac a new era begins for humanity. These astrological eras reflected in the signs of the zodiac are therefore directly tied with different historical epochs. When looking back over the epochs of the past, we can see clearly that certain cultures rose and fell with these astrological ages reflected by the zodiac.

The duration of an astrological age is about 2,000 – 2,500 years. All ages are equal in length and follow each other in a backward motion. An entire cycle of 12 ages that correlates with the 12 signs of the zodiac lasts roughly 26,000 years. Additionally, this Zodiac Cycle parallels the Great Galactic Cycle's duration. Although from a linear point of view these two cycles differ somewhat in length, in the end they are parallel. This calculation is of a more esoteric nature, and cannot be grasped with the tools of logic.

The complete cycle of the zodiac symbolically represents the entirety of human consciousness. Thus, with the terrestrial movement through time and space the total paradigm of human experience is worked through within a time frame of approximately 26,000 years. After the completion of a Zodiac Cycle the archetypes begin to repeat themselves. Evolution then takes place within similar dynamics put in the context of new circumstances and different issues.

Geometrically, human evolution transpires in circles or more precisely, in spirals. The third dimension representing depth ensures that the same position in the circle is worked out again and again, each successive time from a different and more developed level. The meaning associated with the astrological signs changes in each cycle. Over great length of time the specific forms of collectively experienced human attributes are modified. Hence, we can only judge accurately within a certain documented time frame. Since the ability to observe and correlate past a specific point in history is not possible, we do not know how the previous times were linked with human experience relative to archetypes and astrological signs. Nevertheless, taking the present and the recent past as the points of reference, this method gives us a very useful and accurate perspective of history in the time- and space-based existence here on Earth.

Many people are familiar with the fact that at this present time we are undergoing a transition of the ages. More specifically, time is progressing from the Piscean Age to the Aquarian Age. Generally, the shift from one astrological age to the next takes place within approximately 500 years. The transition time "borrows" qualities from both, the preceding as well as from the new age. It will still take a few hundred years before the Aquarian Age will be firmly established. During the transition from one age to the next, all the issues from the past 2,000 years linked with the collective mode of operation and the prevailing belief systems are coming to a head. In order to resolve these issues they are brought forth with great multitude.

The succeeding paragraphs focus on the description of the astrological ages. This will help to supply the background for a broader view and deeper understanding of this current transition. Seen in a larger context the transition adds a unique perspective and offers a resolution specific to this time. It brings in hope and light for a future that is not based on the past, but rather on letting go of it, while henceforth embracing change. This requires courage to allow the unknown to exist and to build on individual as well as on collective present circumstances. The indications, hints, repeated clues, and suggestions we receive through creative thoughts, insights, or flashes of intuitive knowing urge us to create a new reality. This reality could be quite spectacular and unprecedented.

In the following description of the astrological ages no presumption or attempt to add to the already existing erudite historical data and research is made. Far more studied people have given elaborate descriptions, reviews, and categorizations by names, places, and events. Their work belongs to the world's wealthy body of knowledge. Whether factual or allegorical and therefore merely figuratively true, the purpose of the following description is to furnish a comprehensive frame for the unique perspective that will eventually unfold for the reader.

A balance of intuitive and rational thoughts greatly enhances the assimilation of this knowledge. It is certainly not helpful to blindly believe without discrimination. Skepticism often is based on spiritual ignorance, however, and in this context would hinder the reader's understanding. A receptive mind is necessary for this perspective, which is based on timeless truth handed down to us from enlightened saints and sages. Much of this knowledge originated during times far more illuminated and spiritually refined than the present. Consequently, it may be scrutinized and rejected if viewed with the erroneous certainty so classically displayed by convictions based on limited empirical data.

Going back to a time where natural principles were in harmony with manmade laws, we would find ourselves in the Virgo Age around 13,000 BCE. This was the era of maximum peace and serenity. The people of Atlantis, as well as indigenous peoples everywhere lived in accordance with the spiritual values of respect for all life, kinship, sharing of resources, and devotion to the Source. This way of life was closely related to the solid grasp of the subtle levels of existence people then had. It coincided with the light peak of the Great Galactic Cycle.

In the indigenous societies of the past the Earth was worshipped as a Goddess. Women too were considered Goddesses because they were giving birth, and because their body was seen to resemble the Earth. All members of indigenous communities were equal in status, regardless of their role, gender, or age. Children were raised communally. There were no nuclear families. As a matter of fact, people did not know that men contributed to procreation. Children were simply the grace of Goddess. There were times when men and women got together to celebrate the fertility of the Earth in sexual rituals. Since women were associated with the Goddess Earth, these rituals were an expression of reverence for life. Sexual union signified the merging with the divine aspect of nature and contained the descent of spirit into flesh.

People rejoiced through mutual usefulness and shared responsibility. Their sense of togetherness came out of understanding their connection with nature. Individualization was not emphasized, and the concept of ownership did not exist. There was no monogamy the way we know it today. All women of childbearing age menstruated concurrently, which also was celebrated. Specific rites for the males of the community were created to build courage. By experiencing and mastering their fears they grew emotionally independent and learned how to derive their sense of security from within themselves. Through these and other specific rituals pubescent members were initiated into adulthood. This had a very distinct effect in that it allowed the young adults to mature emotionally.

The Age of Leo followed the Virgo Age. It was when the civilization of Atlantis had its final ascension and consequent fall. These people had a very highly advanced technology. Their knowledge and technological abilities were in some ways much more refined than what we have available now. They used their highly cultivated awareness of the subtle energy underlying all manifested forms to invent scientific methods by which matter can be manipulated. Nevertheless, this age was the antecedent of our present time concerning science and technology. Instead of striving toward balance and working in harmony with the forces of nature, people became perverted by the power their abilities gave them. Motivated by self-interest and greed the few were leading the many away from shared resources into misusing their technology. The shrouding darkness in human consciousness relative to the Great Galactic Cycle's progressing phase of contraction is reflected in this development. Inevitably this led to cataclysmic events that destroyed not only the culture, but also the continent.

As an aside remark: to this very day no one really knows how the pyramids and the Sphinx in Egypt actually were built.

These monuments carry erosion marks indicating great amounts of rainfall. This could very well mean that the structures are much older than previously believed. If so, they might have been created during the time of Atlantis, where people utilized very advanced methods enabling the construction of such shrines. One of the theories is that sound technology was employed to move the enormous rocks on these stone monuments. Thus, it is easy to see how the technology of Atlantis was also powerful enough to cause mass destruction.

The fall of Atlantis coincided with the time of the great floods, and brings us into the Age of Cancer. Partial destruction of the planet, with rain, flooding, and other natural catastrophes occurred. These cataclysmic events wiped out most of the previous civilizations in the areas of the Mediterranean, the near East, and possibly along the coastline worldwide. It is as though Goddess wanted to recreate Her creation. This time also corresponds to the story in the Old Testament of Noah and his Ark. Most likely there were areas where people lived untouched by these circumstances. Places such as the elevated areas of the American continents, East Asia, and Australia may not have been subject to change resulting from the catastrophic incidents.

In the areas where human beings were impacted by these events, the cerebral cortex of their brain began to evolve in its rational, deductive capacity. The intense natural disasters forced them to become inventive and resourceful. New dynamics surfaced. It was around this time when the realization emerged that men contributed equally to procreation. As a result the males were compelled to call the child they fathered their own. Eventually they began to enforce this strong point. The women who were giving birth to their children needed to be owned as well. Craving for ownership did not stop there. In order to provide for woman and children it became important to possess land and animals as well.

What followed was a dramatic change in social order from indigenous communities to nuclear families. The shift occurred over millennia during which the main motion of social evolution gravitated toward individuation. Moving away from a sense of coherence and connectedness augmented self-interest and severance in all aspects of life. The heightened feeling of isolation triggered the primal anxiety of separation from the womb each human being encounters at birth. Giving birth along with most other rites of passage lost their communal sense of belonging and organic wholeness. From this point forward children were conceived, born, and raised in the restricted environment of the nuclear family. Over time the sense of division further stimulated the deductive thinking process. Rational thought views and processes everything by being apart from it. This mental mode of operation was cohesive with people's new sense of individuation. At this point it was already fostered from birth and progressively mirrored in all areas of life.

The migration that occurred during the succeeding Age of Gemini also resulted from the great disasters. The people who survived the turbulent Earth changes of the Cancer Age began to migrate in order to find new land and resources. With the different tribes wandering and socializing there was suddenly a new crisis. Fiercer tribes were conquering the more peaceful ones. In many of the areas where human beings were still more or less settled in one place they had kept totally to themselves. These people never even knew that others existed. Consequently, they had no enemies other than nature by way of cold, heat, water, or animals trying to invade their settlements. They saw themselves in union against the natural challenges, and this is where their struggle took place.

Then things changed abruptly. Hoards of foreign conquerors raged through and upset what was once the original settlers' stable world. Due to the natural catastrophes these invaders had become feral. Because their land no longer existed, they were forced to leave their habitat and move out into far-off territory. This was a necessity brought on by their need for survival. Likewise, the original tribes used to being the only people around were faced with a tremendous new challenge. Their struggle for survival also changed in character. Rather than having nature, the elements, and some animals as their only predators, they now had to fight human invaders.

As different ethnic groups were competing for the same land, the same hunting grounds, and the same sheltered areas, war seemed to become a necessary consequence. The collective psyche was echoing with the faint memories of natural disasters of cataclysmic magnitude. With the Great Galactic Cycle moving closer toward its dark peak, materialistic perception continued to increase the sense of division. It was tinted with the consciousness of men fighting men and was reflected in survival strength of powerful possessions and a large clan to outnumber the enemy. By this time the physically stronger and intellectually more aggressive males were the social leaders. They had the superiority over women. Because of their physical strength, male attributes were idolized, cherished, and cultivated. The invention of sky gods followed. Authoritarian concepts became the basis of religion.

During the following Age of Taurus the farming of land and agricultural development flourished. Construction of colossal structures such as the pyramids in Mexico also ensued. These new developments reflected the need for stability and abundance. They suggested people's expression of a distant fear, and seemed to say, "God is on our side, and never again will our land, our home, and our resources be taken away." The soil was cultivated with the use of oxen, hence the image of the bull that symbolizes the Age of Taurus. There was a need to ground and consolidate what had been established. People viewed everything from the perspective of ownership. As human consciousness contracted, the division between natural directives and manmade laws grew. Respect for all life gave way to materialism and acquisitiveness. In some cultures this did not even stop with death. The Egyptian pharaoh's wife, for example, was buried alive with him.

The Roman Empire with its delusive dreams of world dominion and subsequent aggressive expansion coincided with the Age of Aries. Partition grew ever stronger and the notion of dominance and submission took a firm hold in domestic life. Married women in ancient Greece and Rome were expected to keep close to the house. Their duty was to raise the children and to serve their husbands. They were not allowed to go out, to learn about the world, or to have friends of their own choice, let alone to have a profession or any private possessions. During those times the only way for a woman to be autonomous, to own land or a house, or to get an education was to sign a paper that officially declared her to be a prostitute.

The Romans had an extremely sophisticated, well-organized, and successful army. Therefore they began to take everything for granted. In their delusion of grandeur they acted as though their power was omnipresent. Their endless feasts, orgies, and decadent way of life knew no boundaries. Entertainment included spectacular games with gladiators. Eventually the Romans became so debauched that they began to neglect the proper protection and guardianship of their cities. Hence, that which was believed to be impossible occurred: the Roman Empire was conquered and destroyed by intruders. Despite the fact that these barbarians did not even possess a tinge of matching sophistication compared with Roman warfare, they were able to take over. At this point the Great Galactic Cycle had reached its contractive peak.

13. Involution

At the creation point spirit divided itself into matter and conscious life energy. In our universe we can focus on matter or on spirit. These are the complementary poles between which human awareness oscillates during the span of the Great Galactic Cycle. Throughout this most recent cycle the core issue in human development is the shift to manmade principles that are not in alignment with natural directives. Fueled by human consciousness' habitual gravitation toward matter, the ensuing consequences of imbalance still increase by the decade.

Harmony prevailed during the light peak of the Great Galactic Cycle, which is approximately 14,000 years ago. People's basic sense of reality was not solely dependent on sense impressions derived from material existence. Their consciousness transcended these tangible realms and included an awareness of astral and causal worlds. As the descending phase of the Great

Galactic Cycle progressed from the spiritual age toward the age of matter, human consciousness began to shift. More and more qualities of discrimination were lost.

First the ability to perceive the spiritual laws of the universe dissipated; then the ability to comprehend the electromagnetism of the subtle energy underlying matter and form was gone as well. Ignorance relative to the atomic structure of elements and the energetic composition of matter followed. The physical side of life became the restricted, yet ever-more-prevailing truth. Only that which was immediately apparent and rationally evident was considered real. This involution of consciousness directly linked with the increasing disregard of natural directives. Insensibility simultaneously emphasized selfishness, which in turn resulted in unequal distribution of common resources and lack of prosperity amidst plenty. Eventually the outcome was widespread economic depression, a phenomenon unknown to preceding cultures.

In the beginning of the transition to manmade laws, the new way of life added an overwhelming number of unforeseen obligations and duties to peoples' daily lives. The entire social order was uprooted, and the population experienced a tremendous amount of stress. The peaceful equilibrium where all responsibilities of the community were equally shared gave way to a tense new sense of separation and exclusion. Because the effort was no longer communal but individual, people began to live their lives in isolation. For the women this meant that they needed to keep close to the fathers of their children, because external circumstances demanded this dependency. the roles of parenting were subjected to a rigid separation: The males became the authority figures and monetary providers while the females were responsible for the domestic facets. Partition was consistent throughout the entire cultural network.

Pigeonholing male and female genders into rigid roles forbade men to have feminine attributes, and women to possess masculine features. This is an unnatural separation because both feminine as well as masculine characteristics are intrinsic to every soul. It is the balance of both qualities that make up a healthy personality. Although in females there may be a preponderance of feminine aspects such as emotional and nurturing elements, these are not inherently absent in men. Yet, with the artificial pigeonholing those qualities had to be suppressed. The same is true for females who were forced to deny their own masculine traits, such as, for example, mental discernment and assertive action.

With the absence of natural rites of passage people no longer matured emotionally. The lack of esteem for nurturing, care giving, and sharing qualities resulted in an imbalance compensated for by the females. They began to control the emotional sphere and became overprotective. The males were idolized in their physical strength. They were supposed to be strong, and could not afford to yield to emotions. The men relied on the women to provide this essential component. Through the resulting division they grew to be emotionally helpless, demanding, or irresponsible. The communal aspects, on the other hand, were almost entirely in the hands of the males. The women's lack of public authority led to their misrepresentation. Being short of equal rights, they were pushed into the role of a minor whose helplessness rendered them needy. Thus both genders acted out their deficiencies caused by fragmentation. They grew up to raise their children without the former sense of social coherence, and without the emotional nurturing children naturally expect. This generated confusion and displaced emotions.

From that time forward people primarily concentrated on the needs of their nuclear family. In this process some were stronger and more skilled at outwitting others, and those who were able to exploit the weaker members grew ever more powerful. They became the leaders of this new social structure upon which our present Western culture is based. In this system the ability to win intellectually or by physical strength outweighs any sense of equality proportionate to nurturing and care-giving qualities that keep the well-being of the entire group as an utmost priority. The saddest part about this is that these values and ways ultimately lead to the dark phenomenon of war. There is no archeological evidence of violence among human beings before this time of change in the basic social structure.

Since conscious awareness diminished to the material level of existence, this level was emphasized also in the realm of religion. New religions were created to serve those in power. Over many centuries the religious customs eliminated feminine power. Gone were the days of Goddess worship where sexuality was the medium through which spirit was connected with the physical body. The progression from natural directives to artificial laws left sexuality bereft of spirit. The indigenous fertility rites and sexual rituals slowly changed to rigid rules of removed formal procedures.

During the cultural shift priestesses were serving the Goddess of creativity and fertility by tending to the flame in the hearth. This role was a remnant of indigenous heritage. The symbols of their virtue were not virginity or chastity, but self-sufficiency and sexual independence. They sexually united with males who sought a direct contact with the creative power of the Goddess. These rituals still were mixed with traces of ancient customs. Just as in the preceding times all grown members once partook in such rituals, the males who visited the priestesses in the

Greek and Roman temples still did so for the purpose of honoring the Goddess. By rejoicing through a ritualized act of sexual union they celebrated the interplay between spirit and flesh. The priestesses' reason for such union was not personal pleasure, monogamous securing of a mate, or procreation of the species. Their role was to bring the spiritual power of fertility and creativity into practical human proximity.

Gradually a peculiar concept of purity was associated with the priestesses. This notion turned out to be devoid of fertility, creativity, and joy. The only aspect reminiscent of spirit was purification, which in this context served to absolve the sins of males. Through sexual union they sought to cleanse themselves morally.

In the succeeding times the idea of purity developed into a dried up extreme of asceticism. Priestesses were chosen as children from the finest families. As they matured into adulthood, they were required to stay sexually abstinent while serving as vestal virgins. The penalty for disobedience of this rule was very severe. If a priestess was caught having a sexual relationship, she was buried alive. Spiritual sexuality was originally a natural, independently powerful, creative expression. At this point celebrating this infinite power of renewal through physical means was denied and repressed. Both genders suffered from this denial because the ability to honor the Goddess and to celebrate life through an emotional and sexual form of spirituality was lost.

Female sexuality and spirituality as originally linked with the concept of life-giving and care-taking qualities split into the extremes of excluding either spirituality or sexuality. The priestesses and later on the nuns had to denounce the natural aspect of sexuality altogether. Conversely, the prostitute became available for soulless sexual union and physical satisfaction. Although scorned for her audacious vulgarity, she nevertheless replaced the self-sufficient temple priestess with whom the men once partook in spiritual rituals of fecundity and worship.

The power of the feminine could not be replaced by a false sense of purity and denial, or by control or dominion. Since the primal affects of emotional and sexual expression inherent to every human psyche was suppressed, it became the basis for many unnatural behaviors and psychological dilemmas. Sexual practices lost all connection with spiritually meaningful values. Instead, sexuality was now viewed merely as a means to an end, either to generate heirs or to seek pleasure. The latter is merely a self-indulgent escape, a regretful distortion. In this vestige of celebration the flesh is glorified for lack of a sexually connected and emotionally meaningful spirituality.

Involution

Fragmentation turned natural sexuality into functionality and indulgence, which was polarized with dry spirituality. While diverging from natural concepts, the price for individuation was loss of spiritual integrity and physical wholeness. Rites of passage in relation to fertility and childbirth, as well as rituals around sexual maturity and sexual union vanished for both genders. Over time these natural aspects of life were pushed further into recessed taboo areas.

The lack of puberty rites of passage contributed to the confusion around sexuality we find in present day Western cultures. Because these initiation rituals were missing, men as well as women no longer knew their role and proper conduct as sexually mature human beings. The helplessness and bewilderment resulted in unnatural and imbalanced behaviors. Today's role models are frequently unhealthy and superficial at best. What teenagers are exposed to often is left to chance. Most of them do not know what responsible natural sexual conduct is, and how it can be experienced in a safe and mature way. What exactly went wrong and how it could all be improved are questions few ask and even fewer seem to have answers for. With culturally integrated puberty rites of passage these quandaries do not occur, because the progression from child to adult is accompanied by practical education. Grown-ups are not confused, nor are they ashamed.

Healthy role models therefore protect the pubescent members of the community.

If fragmentation, rationalization, and the ensuing sense of isolation are experienced internally, these qualities also are found externally. Acting out the inner reality confirms the existing limitations of consciousness. This in turn supplies self-consistency and security even if it is not beneficial. Along with the feeling of inner isolation, the people during the descending phase of the Great Galactic Cycle began to lack a sense of autonomy. The invention of sky gods, who would punish if their rules were not followed as expected, enforced this sense. While conveniently serving those in power, the thought of these gods' menacing mastery led to an inferiority complex for the common populace. This was entirely conditioned by developments that were not in alignment with natural social and spiritual directives. This inferiority complex could take hold because people heard the same information repeatedly. Finally it became a disempowering belief, even if this belief was not based in truth.

Conditioning of the inner reality on an individual level laid the foundation for a society that was out of touch with natural paradigms. This happened because human consciousness was in a phase of decline relative to its conscious awareness. People's intuition was blunted. They were no longer capable of trusting and validating their own experience. The ease with which they used to tune into their inner sense of knowing was lost. What once enabled their ancestors to act in self-empowered ways had been replaced with blind belief.

Putting these events in the context of the ages of the zodiac, we can see that the descending phase of the Great Galactic Cycle continued through six ages and sub-ages. The decline began in the Age of Leo, followed by the Ages of Cancer, Gemini, Taurus, and Aries. At that point the predator and prey reality of existence predominated. In regard to the decline of conscious awareness and subsequent prevalence of materialism, the Great Galactic Cycle's darkest peak coincided with the Age of Pisces. On all levels, including religion, this was enacted as the survival of the fittest. The notion was that people were superior to nature, and their way of life was the only way. Anyone who thought differently deserved to die. The Crusades and the Inquisition are appalling testimonies of this fact. Humanity became diabolically inspired by exclusively materialistic principles. Evil exaggerates the predator and prey reality and the reality of separation. Tangible effects are the immediate and only gratification.

Although the dynamics began to change direction around 2,000 years ago, at this point in time we are still very close to this exclusively materialistic reality. As a result of conditioning, rational thought is yet winning against intuition in our brains. In many ways the full impact of the descending phase toward involution was never more powerful than it is now. At the same time the light is beginning to shine through many new directions, a sure sign that humanity can no longer be satisfied with exclusively logical and materially oriented principles. The search for intuitive knowing and comfort motivates people to try out new directions.

Looking at it from the point of maximum light equaling twelve o'clock, we are now around seven o'clock in our current Great Galactic Cycle. As we advance toward the increasing light of conscious awareness, natural dynamics are beginning to put a restraint on materialistic identification. This is psychologically irritating for most people, because they desire to keep going in their familiar ways. The need for security is a subconscious motivating factor to recycle the already established patterns.

As the light phase of the Great Galactic Cycle approaches, the whole of creation will give resistance to any force that is not helpful, equitable, and harmonious to all. It is necessary to pause and look at what must be discarded. Natural principles are universally beneficial energies. Exclusion and self-interest will have to give way to these principles. In its natural progression involution is being replaced by evolution. For constructive continuation it is also important to focus on re-embracing ritualistic aspects that have lost their deeper meaning. This will help people in their archetypal transition toward wholeness and personal as well as collective expansion in consciousness.

14. The Age of Pisces

What we require in order to support and maintain our existence is what we value most. Our set of values is directly linked with our beliefs. These beliefs in turn correlate with how we interpret phenomenal reality. Whenever beliefs change, that which constitutes meaning for us changes too. As a result we begin to value different experiences and things. Of course this process also operates the other way around. Different experiences we attract can cause us to interpret reality differently. Thus we create new values and, respectively, our needs are no longer the same either. This alters how we give meaning to our life, and so it happens that we find our beliefs changed as well.

This phenomenon also occurs on a collective level. The same dynamics operate between survival needs, values, and the resulting belief structures, customs, and demeanor of entire families, as well as cultures and nations. Human values differ greatly relative to time and place. What any culture or group of people needs in order to survive determines how the collective value system, including standards and ethics, is shaped, and what is given significant meaning. Beliefs are born out of this collective meaning. They serve to motivate the populace to consciously or subconsciously worship what is perceived as requirements for the functioning of the entire society. Along these lines beliefs can be manipulated.

Religious beliefs too are closely related to the background, circumstances, and conditions of a culture's basic survival needs. When survival needs change, many religious beliefs become redundant; they then hinder collective and individual evolution. Since the Great Galactic Cycles is now in its expansive phase, evolution is the necessary vehicle for progress. Rather than continuing to promote invented beliefs, progress thus occurs through re-aligning spiritual orientation with actual needs and currently relevant requirements. Thus meaning and values match; they become once more authentic.

In order to understand the Piscean Age and its religious beliefs, it is relevant to first look more closely at the collective values and the meaning people had given their lives. The cultures of the more recent epochs progressively emphasized a lifestyle where the few were leading the many. Therefore, survival depended on effective leadership and obedient people. Since people relied on the integrity of the leaders, their values and meaning in this sort of cultural organization were susceptible to abuse. Once the leaders' values began to degenerate into the greed of egotistical exclusion and power-motivated behaviors, the entire culture suffered. During the dark phase of the Great Galactic Cycle the increasing limitations in human consciousness made it impossible to eliminate this evil influence.

Belief systems gradually emphasized a supreme being in the form of one or several authority figures that had to be feared. These metaphysical authority figures had the power to provide fitting answers through an orientation that involved the outer world and logic, but explicitly excluded the inner knowing of intuition. The individual person's spiritual, worldly, as well as social experience was associated with a sense of isolation. It echoed in the way people related to themselves.

The impersonal and unreachable Gods and Goddesses of this time resided in remote places such as temples on lofty mountaintops or in the sky. The concept of the Source moved from an intuitive inner knowing and natural bonding with all of creation to these faraway, all-knowing, controlling, and often also frightful deities. In this way the common masses began to simultaneously feel a deep lack of psychological empowerment. Likewise, the leaders of this new social structure cultivated an appearance imitating that of the supreme beings of these new beliefs. Thus the collective fear originating from lack of spiritual inner resources and deprived emotional sustenance was amplified. It enabled those in power to create superiority, while the populace was raised to obey and follow their orders. The leaders supplied the common populace with their convenient version of what the Gods were conveying. This further prepared the soil for a passively docile morale.

As time went on people were no longer able to tune within to receive spiritual insights that could have helped them find solutions or comfort. They sadly lost all sense of self-reliance, while their inner autonomy was replaced by a subdued mindset of oblivion. The common citizens were now looking to their religious leaders for answers their ancestors would easily have found themselves. Bit by bit the collective unanimously accepted beliefs that supported their unquestioned inferiority and obedient submission. Religion had become a political tool. This contrivance served the leaders' self-interested agendas.

Any centralized system is dependent on the functioning of its hub. Corruption of leadership is an inherent danger with this type of social order. The systems of the Greeks and the Romans, for example, were tailored to the needs of the leaders for their own sake, and often not for the good of all. The common citizens compensated for the expansive appetite of their megalomaniac leaders. The "spiritual" inspiration these cultures drew from Gods and Goddesses was a mirror image of this social climate. Many of their deities were endowed with dreadfully ostentatious characteristics that lacked sincerity, wisdom, mercy, and accurate judgment. These were precisely the values the dominant part of the leadership held.

Since these cultures' collective needs were no longer truly replicated by their leaders' actions, the religious as well as the social structure lost their integrity. These systems degenerated relatively quickly owing to the increasingly fiercer materialistic inclinations, ferocious appetites, and pompous, egotistically expansive desires of the ruling class. The involution of consciousness caused exploitation, widespread economic imbalances, famine, illness, rampant competitiveness, and war.

The dynamics of the Great Galactic Cycle's dark peak show how the delusion of acquisitiveness also took hold in the religious orientations of their times. Although clearly counterproductive, these values were holding true past their dark time of climax. A life out of balance impeded on the welfare of the people. Dysfunction took hold in the psyche in ways no one could even recognize as such. The effects of these belief systems increasingly spread like an uncontrollable cancer, and they are to a large degree still operative today.

The dark culmination of the Great Galactic Cycle occurred around the shift to the Piscean Age. Through complementary polarization, darkness contains the light as a seed potential. In all times of intense struggle and strife the Great Spirit sends a self-realized soul to Earth. The purpose of this enlightened being in ordinary human form is to help the fraught people to seek their way back to truth, love, and healing. At the beginning of the Piscean Age Jesus was such a harbinger of light and love. He taught with the use of parables to help people regain their inner sense of intuition, which would set them free. He directly trained only a select handful of disciples. Most people did not understand what he was saying, and later on his teachings were grossly misinterpreted and misunderstood.

At that time the Romans occupied the Holy Land. The Jewish people were hoping for the Messiah, someone who would show them the way to God, and would liberate them from their subjugation by the Romans. Before this time there had been many false Messiahs, and due to this betrayal of their trust, people's ears were no longer receptive. For this reason Jesus in the end became the prophet who was not recognized in his own country. Of course he had many followers. He taught by example and was committed to the truth above and beyond outdated, empty customs. Because he was not dogmatic nor did he follow any tradition blindly, there were also those who opposed him. Jesus was not willing to perform miracles to satisfy people's cravings for sensational events. What is more, he exposed those who performed their religious customs hypocritically. Therefore, the Pharisees wanted him killed.

The Romans did not know what to do with Jesus, so they gave the people a choice about whether he or the murderer who was waiting for his execution should go free. They released the murderer and Jesus was crucified. Although he could easily have avoided this hardship, he did nothing. He reacted with nonviolence in the face of ignorance, hatred, and vengeance, thus proving that the power of love is stronger. It was his way of pointing out the futility of fighting evil with evil, confirming that violence is of the same mold. Jesus said that all those who take the sword should perish with the sword. His faith in the Great Spirit and his infinite soul carried him through the sacrifice of his body. He knew that through this final test of surrender his soul would gain ultimate liberation from earthly incarnations.

Jesus also knew that the most powerful way to teach others was to follow the trend of his time. The unspeakable atrocity of his crucifixion was in fact a way to teach people at the dark peak of the Great Galactic Cycle how to learn from their mistakes in hindsight. Jesus became the scapegoat of his time, an enlightened being persecuted and sacrificed, a victim of the dullness that ruled the collective mind. How to act with foresight rather than realizing the outrage in hindsight is one of the core lessons of the Piscean Age. To this very day we are still grappling with this lesson, and in many ways it has even intensified.

During the succeeding centuries the people who disseminated Jesus' teachings eventually ended up forcing others to their own way of life. In their delusional hypocrisy they used the wrong means and the wrong reasons to disseminate the teachings of the Piscean Age. Confusion along with victimization, blame, and persecution has continued to ripple through the past 2,000 years. The message of light contained within Jesus' teachings was sadly lost in the thinking of domination. The fanatical religious tendencies of today's world attest to this fact. When people do not have an inner conviction, but depend on dogmatic outer beliefs, converting others symbolizes the security they seek. Self-righteousness, religious extremism, or materialistic motivations can never justify inhumane means. Using confusion to win people for unjust causes is only possible when they themselves do not know what is inherently right and wrong.

In societies where people are out of touch with natural directives, uncertainty, mystification, and misunderstanding prevent them not only from seeing the truth about right behavior but also from healthy living. They carry afflictions for which no one seems to have any cure. Today there are medical and psychological descriptions as well as drugs to help stabilize depression and various other imbalances. Support groups for virtually every addiction and for an almost endless multitude of contemporary disorders are available for those who suffer acutely. More often than not, however, healing does not occur. As long as disease consciousness rules the mind, health is merely an abstraction of wishful thinking. Without understanding how the deviation from natural principles created confusion, imbalance, and unnecessary suffering it is not possible to effect any permanent healing. Once we touch down to the bottom line of the actual causes for modern dysfunctions, a path of action for their healing can follow.

15. Creation Myths

Creation myths are intrinsic to human existence; they delineate our origin with various parables. Just like the different gods of many cultures, the specific framework of the civilization that generated them binds creation myths. Their substance and authenticity rely on timeless wisdom and eternal truth. There is an important distinction to be made when determining the validity of a creation myth.

What is inherently natural belongs to the realm of life principles and is eternally and unalterably true. Myths derived within a time frame where humans were in touch with these natural life principles therefore possess significance that exceeds the culture from which they originated. In myths where there is little timeless essence present, temporary laws and customs laid the foundation for their interpretation. Many of these laws were not in alignment with natural principles; hence they come and go with the rise and fall of their culture. It is therefore important to analyze the context within which a myth was created. We can then objectify its content and draw relevant and practical conclusions.

During the Great Galactic Cycle's phase of involution people have no ability to inwardly realize the transparency of how spirit solidifies into matter and vice versa, nor do they possess the supernatural capacity to affect such alchemical processes. Although they do not have these skills, human consciousness always possesses the power to create as the Source does. It can manifest when the personal will is aligned with divine will.

Through creating many forms from the one spirit, the Source fulfilled a desire to project itself into the manifested universe. With this each soul became an individualized, yet inseparable part of spirit. Each human being is capable of remembering this spiritual origin through continuous conscious effort. People naturally lose sight of this during the contractive phase of the Great Galactic Cycle. In this loss we may be able to recognize the need for creation myths. They are meant to inspire us to see our own astounding potential to be whole. During the light peak of the Great Galactic Cycle people inwardly realize this ideal and tend to consciously strive toward it on an individual basis.

The loss of human omniscience is rooted in the ultimate involution that occurred through the energy moving out from the

Source. The Universal Source "caused" this loss by the sheer act of projecting itself into matter and consciousness. Matter is never perfect, but human consciousness evolves in various cycles of expansion and contraction through a step-by-step process toward the perfected state of enlightenment. The cycles of involution and evolution pertaining to the Great Galactic Cycle coerce human souls to realize their limitless consciousness, which they naturally "forgot" because of the original separation from the Source. The loss of spiritual omniscience can be seen as a chance at evolution, where this state is recovered through gradual improvement.

We know from those who walked the path to illumination that Goddess guided human beings to return to Her through the expansion of consciousness, and not through seeking perfection in the finite world of matter. The only way to reach perfection is to embrace life as it is and to grow with it. We can overcome our human shortcomings and differences with love. The grace that stems from accepting limitations leads to their metamorphosis. In order to realize this, we need to be in touch with life's natural directives through our intuition.

Throughout the ages humans needed a way of explaining how their state of omniscience was lost in the first place. Longing to merge with the Source is rooted in the archetypal unconscious, and simultaneously with other desires influences our actions and our perception. This is where religion and all spiritual teachings originate. Although there may be no creation myth that is factually true, those that are based in natural directives convey timeless messages of wisdom. Let us now examine a myth that shows how the contracted consciousness of the dark phase of the Great Galactic Cycle created confusion and negative emotional states. In contrast to creation myths developed through natural directives, the biblical story of Adam and Eve was seen through principles of its time.

Because of their disobedience to God's directives Adam and Eve were forced to leave the Garden of Eden. According to the myth this is how the first two human beings lost paradise. Loss and longing are very closely linked. From a psychospiritual point of view, the loss of paradise and the longing to merge with the Source are essentially the same. They both represent our desire to be whole and perfect, to be relieved of our human limitations, to be united with spirit. Loss is oriented toward the past; longing is directed toward the future. The difference is that the past is unalterable, while the future can be influenced by the present.

Alignment with the past generates concern with the feeling of loss. This often results in a need to blame this loss on someone or something. Combined feelings create new feelings or whole new concepts. For example, loss and the resulting feeling of grief combined with anger easily can generate vengefulness. Loss combined with understanding enables metamorphic change that leads to growth.

The combination of two negative feeling states will produce a new feeling state limited by that same negativity. The combination of a negative state with a positive one such as understanding creates progress through compassion. Instead of the stagnation that occurs when blaming someone or something for the loss, healing takes place through letting go. Understanding life as a series of transformational opportunities where nothing and no one is taken for granted brings about the needed momentum to move forward. The negative state of loss is linked with the positive quality of compassion. Blame never enters the equation.

When the story of Adam and Eve is told from a viewpoint that is entrapped in bondage to matter, its orientation is toward the past. The contained allegorical truths of this parable are then biased toward loss, anger, and blame. This limits its significance and value. Corresponding to the involution of consciousness that took place at the time this story emerged people experienced lack of clarity on all levels. Blind belief made it easy to be misguided. Because they were disconnected from their own inner natural direction, these people were suffering from isolation. The lack of depth in rituals and initiation rites further reflects this fragmentation. The memory of lost intuition was linked with negative feelings that created the need for blame.

Goddess' guidance for Adam and Eve was not to eat the apple from the tree in the middle of the garden. Adam and Eve did not heed Goddess' warning, and the fall from grace occurred. How could it not? As human beings they were of course subject to human sensations. The loss of paradise was interpreted as caused by these two. The concept of perfection further falsified the message of this myth. It generated the need for blame, because Adam and Eve failed to be perfect as judged from an illusory standard of conduct. The loss was seen as a direct punishment from God. This orientation toward loss induced guilt. It resulted from those manmade laws that are antagonistic to life's natural principles. The inability to take responsibility for their humanness by creating an unnatural concept of sin out of this loss was a perceptual error.

The Garden of Eden myth also gives these dynamics of loss and blame male and female characteristics. It interprets how the fall from grace occurred in this context. Evil in the shape of a snake tempted Eve to take the fruit from the forbidden tree in the center of the garden. Eve gave in to the snake that was enticing her with the famous apple and she seduced Adam to eat from it as well. As a result the first two human beings were cast out of the garden. On a symbolic level the fruit on this tree represented their sexuality. In their human form they were tempted by this energy. This is only natural. Even so, there was simply no conscious power available to link feelings in a way that would have sustained natural directives and awareness of actual truths. People demanded unreal perfection because they had forgotten what it means to be human.

In man-made religious beliefs sexuality and emotions became directly linked with this concept of original sin. Along with the artificial tenet that it was wrong to engage in sexual behavior, it was the basis of unnatural guilt resulting from a natural phenomenon beyond these people's control. The natural sexual impulse was enticing to both genders above and beyond the fact that it was also the vehicle for reproduction. Although it was tempting, it now had to be resisted.

Because resisting these tempting impulses was virtually impossible, it resulted in a sense of powerlessness in the face of nature's principles. The inherently natural sexual attraction truly was stronger. The catch of course was that they were compelled to feel guilty for this phenomenon. Although the guilt people experienced around their sexuality and emotions was not natural, it was real. Not only had they lost their connection to spirit, they had also lost their inherent right to feel good about being part of the natural creation. Everyone was experiencing inadequacy and helplessness. People's coping mechanism became distorted, which created much suffering.

The story of Adam and Eve also can be interpreted from a point of natural directives. This is where we find its timeless value. The following interpretation of the Garden of Eden myth supports the loss with an orientation toward the future and positive development. When they lived in the Garden of Eden, Adam and Eve possessed the ability to transform their spiritual ideas into material existence. Goddess endorsed these creatures with elements from both the animal kingdom as well as from the subtle astral realms. Within the latter, supernatural aptitude was an integral component. This ability to create manifested forms out of spirit was possible, because these human beings were in direct contact with the sacred metaphysical aspects of their own nature. They realized the partial and therefore illusionary dream reality of their earthly existence, and in this expanded consciousness they were able to maintain their unity with spirit. This was a permanent state of joy and peace beyond the relativity of sensory impressions in the world of complementary opposites.

This does not mean that Adam and Eve were not loving life on the physical plane, but merely that their mental composure and self-controlled evenness to the feelings evoked by sensory stimuli granted them constant inner calmness and serenity. Spiritual attunement in conjunction with sense enjoyment that was directed by wisdom and freedom from craving pleasure guided all their conscious actions. They were naturally devoted to the subtle forces of creation, preservation, and dissolution through which the everlasting and unalterable Great Spirit works in the universe.

For Adam and Eve the ego had no selfish bearing on their behavior. Through devotional qualities they were able to maintain ongoing contact with their spiritual lineage. They successfully controlled their senses, instincts, and their basic performance of manual dexterity, movement, and procreation. They knew how to listen to the Infinite Spirit speaking to them through their intuition. This was paradise as this myth describes it.

Conversely, on planet Earth the fluctuation of consciousness tested Adam and Eve's own free will. This is how the loss of their supernatural power and intuitive resonance with spirit occurred. The human prototype's original omniscience became obscured. It was subject to gravitational influences, delusion, and temptation. Adam and Eve thus naturally began to follow worldly ways. This included the laws of physical procreation through the base instinct of sexuality, which was the way the animals reproduced their species. Since Adam and Eve's bodies had evolved from these forms, they then remembered their physical ancestry. Their consciousness became centered on physical existence.

The Garden of Eden is a metaphor for our potential. On planet Earth the basic human make-up is half deity and half animal, another complementary pair of opposites. All people are required to work on the connection with their divine qualities. Because the Source is not perfect in its manifested aspect, but also evolving, these qualities can only be developed through an ongoing, conscious cooperation with this Source. Through mastering the interplay between spirit and matter, human beings will eventually find their way back to the Garden of Eden, where they will rise above the physical laws of existence.

In the above interpretation the vehicle of sexuality is merely chosen as an example, because it contains the most compelling sensual component. This is by no means the only way people's self-control goes off the rails in the world of matter. Attachment to physical existence always causes humans to forget to strive toward their divine origin. The Great Galactic Cycle's phase of involution additionally causes spiritual ignorance. Most humans do indeed experience themselves separate from spirit. Through the second interpretation of the Garden of Eden myth we understand this separation intrinsic to earthly existence. The resulting limitations, attachments, and evil influences along with some of the ways they can take hold are the cause of our loneliness. On the positive side they also spur our love for others and for the Source. Explaining the loss of paradise without blame creates a natural frame within which to place the dynamics that brought on this loss; indeed, they are inherent to creation. The myth's positive interpretation is a key to growth. It puts humanity to work in the realm of their spiritual evolution.

In the context of the times the myth was conceived, its interpretation was not constructive. The dynamic of blame disempowered people. It was also a convenient justification to fault the women for the loss of paradise. These were the times when the social structures had shifted, and fabricated laws served the purpose of male domination. In the parable Eve was associated with emotions, sexuality, and the body, along with the passive and receptive energy related to the weakness of giving in to temptation. Eve was accordingly denounced as being akin to evil. Since feminine aspects were linked exclusively with females, women could be blamed for the entire dynamic. The rationalization went from female to sexuality, emotions and the body, then to temptation, and, finally, to evil.

In this interpretation of the myth it is interesting to note that despite the association of the masculine principle with reason and right judgment, there is no acknowledgment of the fact that

Adam's decision to taste from the apple was his choice, made of his own free will. Adam is portrayed as the victim of Eve's seductive powers of persuasion. It was convenient to blame the female for succumbing to temptation and corrupting the male to the lowly actions of the emotions and the flesh. As the men fell prey to the same natural dynamics, the myth served as an outlet for their own bewilderment. In reality they too suffered from an inner lack of connection with life's natural orders.

The way to deal with the imagined guilt that resulted from the myth was either to reject it or to embrace it. Rejecting it became coupled with anger. The negative feelings of guilt and anger combined in this way created an effective weapon of fault finding. Those who gravitated toward this mode punished others for the unnatural feelings of shame and deep sense of inadequacy they felt from within their own psyche. They experienced themselves as the helpless victims of dynamics that were stronger than they were. Accordingly, they acted out their inadequacies and subconscious guilt in a false sense of righteousness. They therefore never consciously reflected on the fact that it was wrong to act this way.

Those who were accused began to feel blameworthy for something for which they were not truly accountable. They instinctively took responsibility for the accusation that there was something wrong with them. This reflected their own inner guilt. They adopted the negative self-image and disapproving values that rationalized their feeling of inferiority. Just as those motivated to be angry and to blame, they were compelled to atone on a conscious, and later on a subconscious level. They began to experience thoughts that progressively foiled their self-esteem. This happened in different degrees of intensity.

All the dynamics described above are not only complex but also essentially dysfunctional. In essence the Garden of Eden myth is not the origin of these patterns, lack of alignment with natural principles is. The accordingly interpreted version of the myth shows how the twisted psychological behaviors lead back to imagined guilt. It resulted from rigid doctrines of artificial perfection and classification into good and evil life aspects. This also included the idea that humans are invariably separate from God. This God expected the suppression of all so-called "evil" realms of existence. Emotional reaction, awareness and expression, the natural response to sexual attraction, and the conscious relationship with the human physical body all had to be denied. The feeling content within human experience became suppressed, hence falsified and distorted.

The suppressed natural instincts were not just going to vanish into thin air. Because the energy continued to have an effect, and this effect was repressed within the conscious mind, it found its outlet subconsciously. Instead of being expressed in their natural form, many human functions were converted into dysfunctional behaviors. Warped concepts, taboos, and rigid sets of conduct caused the examined unhealthy patterns of guilt, dominance, and submission. For many people they also brought on a deep inner sense of meaninglessness resulting in a wide array of abnormal behaviors including compulsions, addictions, and escape into fantasy or hedonism.

During this descending arc of the cycle from light into darkness people were particularly concerned with evil, greed, temptation, blame, and justification for power. The Garden of Eden myth builds on these patterns to point the blame in the direction it was most convenient. Those who had power used it for self-interested purposes. The myth justified the status quo and supported the delusive stance with which they were afflicted. In this is illustrated once more how values are linked with meaning. Since they valued their exclusive power, the belief systems were adapted to supply a meaning that fit their needs. It gave people the self-appointed right to keep others down. They boosted the idea of catering to a perfect God, whose expectations could never be lived up to, and who was not pleased unless one denied a part of one's inherent nature. Compassion with one's own and others' imperfections was replaced by harsh judgment.

Instead of seeing the Source as an evolving force, most people consistently lost out against this stifled concept of soulless perfection. The deeper the natural aspects of human existence had to be buried, the more falsification was created. This included the loss of all forms of emotional spirituality. To reiterate an important point: the notion of perfection within earthly existence was created by cultures that were no longer connected with the intrinsic roots of existence. In alignment with life's natural directives perfection is a concept that reflects our inner orientation. Falling short of ideals is human; it is the striving toward them that needs encouragement. There is a close affinity between our actions, intentions, and desires. Perfection lies in the ability to inwardly perceive and accept the true nature of our desires. Real faultlessness is being able to openly convey this to others in a sincere way. The purity of specific motivations, intentions, and actions depends on this inner orientation, not on an invented outer concept of ultimate perfection.

Integrity of motivations and sincerity of action belong to an emotional form of spirituality. If we are to be happy and fulfilled, we need to understand that perfection is part of the soul's secret wish to merge with spirit. Dishonesty with self or others only increases the stance of separateness, and so does lack of compassion with our perfectly human imperfections. Merging arises with successful expansion of conscious awareness through some form of sacred practice. It can never occur through any type of man-made law based on dogmatism or distorted psychological perceptions.

PART THREE

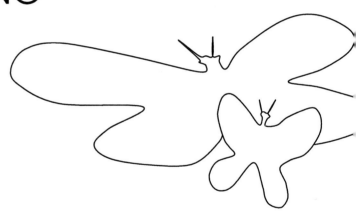

EVOLUTIONARY

HEALING

16. Dedication and Resistance

When the focus is on healing, the subject oversteps the boundaries set by customs, norms, standards, and taboos. We often are unaware of our idiosyncratic behaviors and of many considerations pertaining to what we cherish. This is especially true also for all the circumstances and values that involve cultural functioning and religious beliefs. When it finally becomes clear that something is obsolete, we may find ourselves still invested in defending it. Observing with detachment becomes necessary. It permits the ability to stand apart from preconceived notions. In evolutionary healing it is vital to look at taboos, those areas avoided and pushed into the recesses of our subconscious. These are the enigmatic issues that dictate patterns of behaviors, ideas, convictions, and judgments through presumed routine and fixed rules. By otherwise disapproving looks, deliberate contempt, or censorship the implied proscriptions are enforced. We learn to avoid any action, thought, or verbal expression that belongs to this restricted area. Because of the amount of energy we invest in quelling them, this restricted area gains power. Harmony gives way to imbalance, and disease follows. In the end the very thing we are trying to avoid stares us in the face.

Guilt is an important function of our conscience. It is the inner barometer indicating to us that something we did was wrong. Guilt is the response to actions that deviated from an internalized norm of right behavior. Whether this standard of conduct is natural or invented does not matter. As soon as consciousness accepts that an action was wrong, the dynamic of guilt is set in motion. The inner judgment is instinctive. The important distinction to make in the context of this process is whether the internalized criterion of proper actions is aligned with life's natural directives, or whether it is an invented, manmade concept. In the latter case, the guilt is not really based on performance that deviated from natural life-governing principles. Despite the fact that its consequences are the same, this guilt is imagined, a constructed, misguided notion that fools people to live in a self-created prison. Once this pattern is established, and culturally accepted, it becomes subconscious and automatic.

An example for a standard of judgment based on artificial principles would be the notion that what we feel about a particular situation is less important than what we think about that same situation. This could be anything–accepting a job offer, taking a trip, entering a new relationship, and so on. If our feelings are persistent, we will begin to experience guilt in this context. This guilt is imagined. Most likely it will result in overriding the feelings and simultaneous acceptance of our thoughts, even if these thoughts lead to wrong decisions or actions that are counterproductive. In this case the feelings represent the instinctive response, the thoughts the culturally conditioned norm according to which we are supposed to behave. If on the other hand the criterion of judgment is based on a transgression against life's natural directives, the guilt is real and unalterable. This guilt too will have an effect, which is necessary to alarm us to our wrongdoings. Examples for such transgressions are premeditated murder, deception to gain power, or stealing for greed. These actions are wrong in whatever society and time they are committed.

During the dark phase of the Great Galactic Cycle distorted concepts of artificial conduct stifled people's natural being. Together with the contemporary myths interpreted to use humanness as sin, they generated an indistinguishable sense of imagined guilt. It led to confusion between genuine suffering that is a requirement for soul growth and artificial, needless suffering.

The indistinguishable sense of shame that caused needless suffering was either resisted while coupled with anger, or it was embraced in eagerness to atone. Passed on over many generations, these dynamics were entirely subliminal. Their influence pervaded all aspects of inner and outer life.

It is true that spiritual progress is based on gaining mastery over sense-based inclinations. With inner discipline and adherence to right action and living, this happens over many lifetimes of psychological battle with worldly attachments. No control or mastery, however, is achieved by denial. Resistance to temptation is vastly different from denial. Although they can look like the same thing from the outside, resistance to temptation is based on restraining superfluous sense gratifications of ego-based desires. This does not mean that soul-based desires are denied at any time. Satisfying those desires that are necessary for the fulfillment of the soul's genuine cravings is of paramount importance. Evolution takes place through metamorphosing limitations, not through suppression.

By disowning and rejecting emotions and the senses, the religious beliefs of the Dark Age were not moving people along the path of evolution. These dysfunctional patterns of behavior generated psychological wounds that to this very day have not been healed. Because they are so intrinsic to modern culture, they are not seen and evaluated in their proper context. Even the current psychological experts fail to recognize the origin, depth, severity, and extent to which these patterns are tied with modern values, beliefs, and habitual behaviors. Because they are viewed from within cultures based on the very principles that generated these misconstrued dysfunctions, no healing is possible. Once the false fabricated concepts are consciously recognized, we can purge them.

It takes much time and effort to uncover the multitude of layers that finally bring liberation from adapted patterns and beliefs. The conditioning of unnatural guilt and suffering is linked with two major subconscious reactions: either resignation and compliance or defiant resistance. The first reaction results in a perceived necessity for submission through atonement. It creates more unnecessary suffering. The second reaction is resistance through mentally cruel or aggressive actions to secure control. This creates more unnecessary suffering as well. Resistance can also express itself in emotionally immature and self-centered behavior.

During the past two thousand years there was no way of consciously identifying these dysfunctional behaviors, as they were part of the very material that wove the cultural fabric. If we are to make progress now, it is crucial to see these ingrained cultural and psychological deficiencies for what they are. With the perspective gained from the Great Galactic Cycle we are able to put them into the context of their origin. Once we understand the cause within this context, it becomes apparent that these aberrant and deeply rooted habitual patterns need to be obliterated. This in turn entails the conscious choice to act differently on a moment-to-moment basis.

On our way out of the Piscean Age the future holds a bright promise of liberation. Yet, the status quo is still influenced by the tendency to look backward. Rather than being motivated to move forward, we are preoccupied with the past in an unusually strong way. Needless to say, this backward orientation is not helpful. The past is not holding the clues for the present, nor is it in any way indicative of future action and events. On the contrary, it perpetuates the dysfunction.

Evolutionary healing puts the feelings of unnatural concepts, imagined guilt, and unnecessary suffering into proper perspective. It is indeed necessary to first look at the past, which is one of the main objectives of this publication. Once this perspective is gained, there is no further need to keep looking backward in countless attempts to recap what never can be changed. The realization that the driving force is an artificial conditioning frees the consciousness from looking into the past and adjusts it to being right here in the moment. Applying the new insights in the present sets the course for permanent change. Instead of analyzing the past, the path of right action is now based on discrimination, evaluation, and instant right choice making. This strategy of liberating from dysfunctional patterns alters the subconscious mind from guilt-driven thinking to self-empowered living. Thus healing from the emotional wounds that produced stagnation can occur.

In the beginning of the process evolutionary healing uses the wounds themselves as a resource. To make their nature conscious is key to identifying the specific psychological affliction. The next phase contains a way out. The final step is to follow through with the self-governing motivation to change and to consistently make the right choices.

Evolutionary healing can be accomplished through understanding the dynamics described here. Through practical observation it is helpful to identify how they work in one's own psyche. The various manifestations of these dynamics play out in an almost infinite array of ways. We can see them first and foremost in personal and professional relationships, but also in the way we relate to work, money, time, possessions, our own body, emotions, and all other issues pertaining to our individual values. Last, but not least, they also play out in the religious or spiritual beliefs we hold. Once the areas and ways these patterns operate are identified, we can release the afflictions they create through choosing new ways of acting and behaving in the face of the old dynamics and surroundings. Instead of looking backward, this offers a way to embrace the present as the stepping stone into the future.

People continue to be confronted with the reality of what they actually encounter, not with invented human beliefs based on unnatural concepts that lead to guilt and confusion. This is the time when human beings need to wake themselves from their delusive slumber of fabricated belief systems. It is necessary now to realize that we have created an inner and outer world mired with needless suffering, aggression, or denial that resulted in the suppression of legitimate needs and natural human functions. As we will see, pointless subliminal suffering has become acceptable or even desirable, while at the same time natural and intrinsic suffering is seen as pathology. The following analysis of resistance and dedication to suffering sheds light on the confusion of natural and unnatural emotional responses.

For the process of healing an attitude of surrender is necessary. We can influence only the process, but never effect the healing itself. All healing in the end is spiritual. When trusting a person, a team, or a process such as prayer to effect healing, surrender is an essential dynamic. In order to surrender we need to submit to something larger than ourselves. With focus, trust, devotion, and faith we allow room for external or internal metamorphosis. When we surrender a shift happens from anguish, separation, misery, and suffering to relief, healing, and wholeness.

When a situation is beyond our control, renunciation of the ego's biased and stubborn stance along with acceptance of limitations can bring about reversal of the situation at hand. All issues pertaining to personal growth involve this dynamic, as well as all processes of healing. By letting go the antidote of comfort is found at the core of suffering. The moment the ego yields its aspirations, desires, doubts, and worries we allow the process to complete itself. Instead of an active, forceful, or dominant stance that resists or interferes with the inherent natural workings, submission is letting go into surrendering that brings salvation. The time of healing is not up to us, but is dependent on the process itself.

A similar process of surrendering is also present in the healing trance of a skilled and experienced shaman working on behalf of a sick person. Spiritual progress too has at its core a certain kind of ego sacrifice, a surrendering of the habitual way of perception and experience. In spiritual or religious worship there is usually a time when the devotees bow, kneel, or even touch their forehead to the floor in reverence. This ritualistic gesture shows evidence of surrender and obedience to a higher power. It becomes apparent in deep meditation as well. Once the everyday habitual mode of thinking has been thrown off successfully, the door to intuitive perception opens. This can lead to a spiritual breakthrough. The dynamic of letting go in relationship to renewal is also found in physiological processes such as falling asleep or in sexual orgasm. In summary, the phenomenon of yielding is intrinsic to life. It is the element of non-action that has the power to transfigure limitations.

Stress is part of life, which is evident even in the world of minerals. Pressurized charcoal, for example, turns into diamond. Fear and pain are inherent elements of the human condition. The child is born only after the mother subjects herself to the labor pain of childbirth. It is evident that a certain degree of dedication to suffering through surrender is necessary to make progress and to heal. What dedication to suffering and surrender consist of is often simply the strength to face things exactly as they are. This is not always pleasant, especially when psychological anguish or humiliation appear to take center stage. Clearly, only a strong person can stand up to this challenge.

Along with sacrificing illusions, self-deception, and idealization, metamorphosis takes place through releasing the ego's identification with preconceived ideas. While utilizing the law of reversal, death and rebirth turn resistance into surrender, egotistic desires into soul growth, and suffering into healing. By courageously submitting to the dark recesses of one's mind, mortification churns over the psychological anguish. Dedication to suffering brings light through the alchemical process of transmutation that can carry a burden to victory. Consequently, dedication to suffering is a sign of strength, and resistance to suffering is a sign of weakness.

This paradoxical statement does make sense within certain parameters only. As long as there is insight, healing, growth, or salvation gained in the process, dedication to suffering is beneficial. On the other hand, if no real benefit is reaped from this attitude, dedication to suffering turns into dysfunction, and resistance to suffering becomes the way out. When the scales are tipped in this direction, resistance is needed. This is what the evolutionary healing process consists of.

Subconscious conditioning dramatically limits the individual's capacity to grow. Freeing the psyche from habitual behaviors represents progression toward wholeness. Wherever this dynamic occurs, letting go brings about healing. This is true despite the fact that in some way convention may be opposed. By allowing tolerance that there is no "one right way," countering the prevalent conditions is necessary and unavoidable. In the final analysis, anything that hinders the evolutionary intent to merge, to find oneness with the Universal Source is resistance.

Owing to the underlying fabricated guilt and its dejected repercussions, subliminal suffering from manmade beliefs has become the rule. At the same time the natural condition of suffering arising from genuine life events is considered unacceptable or repulsive. There is a stilted apprehension toward the metamorphosis and transformation intrinsic to natural life processes. This is visible in the unnatural manner contemporary Westerners live and behave. In so many ways life lacks spontaneity and organic coordination. Instead of aging gracefully, for example, many people try to cover up these signs in painful and unnatural ways. This dedication to pain is self-inflicted. It is not caused by nature, but by culturally distorted means.

The fear of death resulting from lack of spiritual attunement with this crucial rite of passage dictates a rigid attachment to the finite form. The sense of self-worth drops in a civilization where youth is glorified at the expense of the wisdom gained through life. Young people too adjust their looks in order to fit a certain superficial mold. They have externalized their values, while the sense of belonging they gain from this becomes an artificial substitute for the absent cultural rituals.

People unconsciously reject many natural phenomena. Artificially induced pain is acceptable, but the inherent distress related to life's transitional stages or any sign of its impermanence is compulsively covered up. This conditioning to conceal overrules all consideration for an organic existence. No one seems to feel that what, who, and how he or she is naturally is good enough. People do not want to comprehend or witness any of life's authentic workings unless they are convenient and feel comfortable. The reason is a deep, permeating manmade shame resulting in the inability to be natural.

Shame and blame generate an afflicted reaction. Compulsively covering up natural truths serves as a fundamental compromise. It tints the most sacred along with the most profane, and converts their meaning. Alienation is the result. While subconsciously compensating for a deep sense of inner inadequacy and emptiness, the illusion of perfection becomes the ultimate conspiracy. It contains as many facets as there are human beings. Unfortunately these facets include harm, sorrow, and suffering that is unwarranted in its core.

These patterns turn life upside down; they reverse its meaning. Natural pain is resisted, and artificial suffering has become a dedication. Pleasure seems to be found in admiring the most successful attempts at outwitting nature. In this contradictory contest the force that turns pain and pleasure into a tailspin is evil. Its game is evident in the English language, where the word "live" spelled backward is "evil."

The confusion resulting from spiritual beliefs that require transcendence of natural life processes has brought on an array of conventions, norms, and ingrained behaviors that prohibit people from knowing who they actually are and what it is they really want. Because change would mean insecurity, they find the most comforting route is to maintain the status quo. The psychospiritual role of the entrenched values and belief systems is to fuel the need for security. This in turn reaffirms the established patterns. In this way people think they know what they are striving for. In fact they are merely scratching the surface of existence while retracing familiar patterns. This behavior definitely does not support the evolutionary needs of most individuals, nor does it serve the more collective needs of the human species at this point in time. Needless to say, it keeps people as far away from the Source as possible.

Those who hold most of this wealth will defend it against all odds. Their beliefs continue to support the old model in the name of a God who is partial to their values. The established wealthy minorities' greed, manipulation, and yearning for power are the breeding ground for illusions the majority of the population is coerced to buy into. Finely clothed in hypocrisy, the hidden agenda of these illusions and delusions uses dangerously corrupt means to an end. At the expense of evolution, and of laws and customs that are equitable to all, involution continues. This is not obvious as long as it is viewed from the point of these firmly established, but truly redundant beliefs and values. Familiarity and habit breed conformity; thus the status quo perpetuates itself. The majority of the people dwell in the past. They prefer to be brainwashed into complacency.

Standing apart from mainstream thoughts and actions will reveal some of the truth. The Great Galactic Cycle, however, supplies an incomparably more meaningful perspective. It takes vast periods of rise and decline and involution and evolution into account. From this comprehensive panorama we can grasp solutions quite adequately. Although not a quick fix, it gives rise to concepts such as evolutionary healing, which motivates dynamic change. Cultural lies sink like rocks in the water when the redundant patterns are worked out in personal self-effort. Intuition develops along with the evolutionary healing process. Once this occurs in a sufficient number of people, collective change can follow. At the present time this perspective is mostly new, unknown, and unrecognized. It will be opposed by the consensus of society because of their security needs for consistency. The comforting thought is that by the time there is no opposition left, we will have passed the collective crossroads for better or for worse, and evolutionary healing in the way it is described here will be obsolete.

The sorrow, pain, and suffering originate from fabricated principles that are not in alignment with life's natural directives. The concept of original sin and its consequent guilt is one important factor in this lack of alignment. At this point this is a redundant, deep-seated neurosis expressed through the unremitting dedication or resistance to suffering. We need to recognize these signs and exonerate the mold that racks people to repeat the fruitless loops of stagnation. It will help clear the path toward regaining an entirely possible and quite practical humanitarian equilibrium.

The growing pains of evolution are a natural occurrence. If any real personal and collective progress is to take place, a certain degree of perseverance is necessary. The growing pains of natural life cycles such as, for example, birth, puberty, childbirth, or death are symbolized in archetypal rites of passage. When examining the rituals of indigenous cultures, a component of painful or metamorphic character often accompanies the event. Purposefully addressing this element of discomfort in their rites of passage is a natural way of accepting and welcoming the challenges, struggles, aches, and difficulties intrinsic to various life stages.

This is vastly different from the more recent distorted avoidance or unnatural dedication to suffering that originates from manmade principles and behaviors. The latter are signs of the time of darkness where materialism is glorified while its repercussions and imbalances are acted out in the psychospiritual realm. Distorted forms of psychological behaviors such as avoidance, resistance, and dedication to unnatural suffering perpetuate denial and illusion. In the artificially imposed limitations of unreal principles we can see the lack of a focus that is naturally spiritual.

When concentrated on and joined with the intentions of the Universal Source, our potential is unlimited. The constant reinforcement of guilt denigrates and devalues our own potential. Returning to natural caliber and appreciation of a transcendent purpose does not mean complete absence of aching transfigurations or human predicaments related to the intrinsic life struggle. Yet it does include an ability to align oneself with spiritual values such as respect for all life including one's own. In the times to come the intrinsic evolutionary pull will highlight the discrepancies along with the necessary changes.

17. Practical Illustrations

As much as suffering is a natural part of the human condition, unnecessary suffering is a poisonous component of which consciousness needs to be purified. In order to purge or neutralize this, we first need to recognize it. Evolutionary healing is concerned with the analysis of these shortcomings and dysfunctions, then with pointing a way out, and finally with supporting and coaching those who desire to move beyond them. In this chapter we will examine the three most prevalent human interactive behaviors that are eminent in today's Western cultures. It is then possible to determine and identify the patterns of subconscious compensation underlying the deep sense of inadequacy that past conditioning has left us to deal with. The following description is meant to provide the reader with an explicit perspective useful in the practical span of life.

Resistance and dedication to needless suffering are two sides of the same coin expressed in three major patterns subliminally pervading every aspect of modern life. These behavioral aberrations have been passed on for many generations; hence their character traits are subconscious, instinctive and self-operating. These phenomena are influencing everyone, not only people who are actively participating in Judaic or Christian religion. Because it is a cultural syndrome, no one's behavior remains unaffected by it. The degree of severity to which it permeates people's psyche, however, varies greatly. It depends on whether an individual's soul in this and/or a previous lifetime was immersed in these religions that propagate rigid doctrines of perfection leading to unnatural guilt and its resulting pathological behaviors.

Healing is in the wound itself. It is of great therapeutic value, therefore, to fully understand in depth the psychological and spiritual dimensions of the defects resulting from artificial concepts as they manifest in various forms. Applying the aspects described here can furnish an understanding of actions and behaviors that to this point were unconscious, or enigmatic at best. The outlined characterizations also will be helpful in the process of personal development. They are meant as guidelines through the maze of worldly, psychospiritual, and social workings.

176

Practical Illustrations

Although these dynamics are modern archetypes and as such are applicable to all, their actual psychospiritual and behavioral manifestations are highly specific. They vary greatly from one person to the next. Regarding the trends of our time, the general principles elaborated here can expand the scope of any healing practice or personal perspective on developmental processes. They have the power to enhance the assessment and understanding of life intentions and circumstances.

Many people who subconsciously experience an excessive artificial sense of guilt instinctively feel a need to atone for this guilt. It motivates them to uphold their dedication to a form of suffering and sacrifice that is uncalled for. Dedication to unnecessary suffering generates the need to find the fault in oneself. Since the guilt is not real, no fault can be found. Still, these people continue to atone compulsively. They waste precious energy in endless loops of compensation trying to live up to some unreal concept of purity and perfection. While in this mode of operation, it is impossible to remove the driving motivation for their truly unwarranted scrutiny.

Artificial guilt linked with unnecessary suffering generates a desire for self-punishment and crisis. Thoughts of worthlessness undermine the primary affirming sense of self-acceptance. Subconsciously they believe that in order to have their needs met they must suffer first. For unknown reasons they think they deserve crisis, pain, and punishment. Although intellectually they know better, they feel useless. Through this conditioning they strive for a warped satisfaction gained from self-punishment and humiliation. People then experience temporary relief from this psychological resignation. Their unreal sense of contentment comes from the wrong impression that through their sacrifice a balance would be achieved. This feeling of false peace derived from atonement further subverts their natural sense of being.

No one can keep sacrificing without gaining something meaningful in return. Since the offerings and sacrifices are made on a distorted basis, no real benefit is reaped. The self-punishment results in a compulsive need to create crisis. These individuals feel victimized by life. The only way to gain any attention is by creating crisis. The crisis, however, often is disconnected from the actual situation. They do not know what prompts the crisis, nor do they have any conscious awareness of how their own desires generate their actions of self-defeat.

The extent to which this distorted psychological condition is present greatly varies. In some individuals it is much more pronounced than in others. People who are afflicted with it need healing. By determining whether any real benefit is yielded, their suffering easily is identified as needless and excessive. Examples of this phenomenon are the workaholic who devotes all of his or her time to the company without asking for, or ever receiving, accurate compensation, and the battered housewife who, despite broken promises from her chronically abusive mate to stop, keeps giving countless second chances.

In these cases the people never get what they need. From their perspective the only way to remedy this state is to maintain it. Nevertheless, they experience an emotional vacuum that leads to a deep sense of inner emptiness. Resorting to some form of crisis becomes their automatic coping mechanism. The inner void is temporarily filled with forced attention, but they have not resolved the underlying dynamic. Although these people suffer, this suffering is self-imposed, a helpless posture that perpetuates an imbalanced situation for lack of deeper understanding. With their artificial martyrdom they avoid real change, while their dejected situation is sustained. Deeply ingrained guilt drives this dynamic perpetually.

Crisis is a stimulus for reflection. It is connected with an ongoing need to analyze the past. Through repetition and deep refection these individuals eventually can learn to identify the cause of their crisis. But unless they are determined, committed to change, and have competent help, it is difficult to fully get to the bottom of this pattern. Because it is deeply ingrained, culturally accepted, and not conscious, it takes an objective perspective that can be gained only by detachment from the underlying cause.

As the cultural background and necessary education relative to the motifs elaborated here has not yet been established, readiness to see and embrace change often is minimal. The dysfunctional behavior is supported by the environment and society in general. Change is either perceived as a threat, or it is not recognized as a viable option. Just as a bird that has been kept in a cage all its life is likely not to fly away, or to return after it is set free, these people act in their habitual ways of age-old subconscious conditioning. Despite cultural sluggishness relative to changing the customary pigeonhole, it is time to step out of this stifling mold. Recent modifications to customs and laws are allowing much more tolerance and equality. Change is now not only possible, but in the face of the apparent dysfunction also urgently called for. In this pattern where suffering is yielded to with atonement the people often respond positively when their behavior is pointed out to them. They can see what it is they are doing. The problem lies in the fact that they often are not committed to doing something about it. This of course is part of the dysfunction. Transformation can occur as soon as the person decides to draw the consequences of the already discerned insights.

Evolutionary healing means gradual shedding of the old skin, while a new one comes into view. When an individual learns to progressively live in the moment and chooses to resist the old pattern of unnecessary suffering through sacrifice and false martyrdom, a healthier pattern begins to emerge. This in turn substitutes crisis with contentment, and submission with self-empowerment. These new aspects in appearance and behavior, although necessary and definitely beneficial, tend to be challenging for the people around the one who is changing. Family members, spouses, friends, or coworkers can become the stumbling blocks. It is important to adjust to the situation by continuing on the path of healing no matter what the feedback may be. Progressively, more and more people will heal these motifs of unnecessary guilt and compulsive need for atonement, sacrifice, and suffering. As natural principles are integrated, society along with its laws also will change gradually. Instead of being alienated in a cultural environment that cannot recognize its own dysfunctions, it will become easier to find compatibility with this healing process.

Because these patterns are so deeply ingrained, the process of changing them takes years to fully complete itself. On a personal level this is so even with resolute steadfastness to change. Culturally it will be many decades, most likely centuries before the dysfunctional motifs are purged completely, and new values and natural behaviors will be integrated. At this point anyone who recognizes and is willing to work out these behaviors can do so within his or her own life. Self-help skills gained from understanding the phenomena described here may be all that is required. If needed, coaching on a sporadic, intermittent, or on an ongoing basis can sustain the process. Over time support will be more readily available, as more and more health care professionals are going to tune into this and similar models of healing.

Resistance to unnecessary guilt and suffering is the flip side of the same coin. The subliminal feelings of shame tracing back to artificial concepts are resisted with anger. The disdainful and sadistic boss whose exorbitant demands torture the already overworked employees, and the controlling mother constantly overseeing and regulating her child who is never allowed to be a child, are examples of this degenerate pattern. Instead of submission leading to an allegiance with redundant suffering, anger is the resistance to that same suffering from unhealthy guilt. Since resistance cannot transmute any emotion, and no true healing occurs without surrender, the submission to suffering has to be projected onto someone else. Consequently, blame is a convenient motivation for this mode of operation.

The anger combined with blame is where much of the instinctively faultfinding and contentious or psychologically cruel behavior has its origin. Since it is subconsciously ingrained as a socially acceptable pattern, it often is not recognized as such. On the contrary, too many people are readily excusing degrading, accusatory, offensive, domineering or insulting conduct as normal behavior. They previously have experienced some form of disdainful, cruel, or abusive actions from a parent, grandparent, extended family member, or educator. By extension they are likely to consider being exposed to the same motif in a professional authority figure or in a spouse as nothing more than uncomfortable. Of course, the displayed behavior may be blatantly obvious and excessively offensive, in which case it would have to be confronted and stopped. However, most of the time the typical circumstances are subliminal or subtle, just not enough to make a scene. Even if disturbed, insulted, or hurt by the behavior, the person affected tends to let it slide. And this is the point: stereotypical dysfunctions are culturally patterned. Although truly abrasive, damaging and degenerate, they run under the surface and are therefore not seen for what they are.

The people with this disparaging behavior attract partners who stoically absorb their cynicism, blame, or cold-hearted withdrawal of affection. In a sense the partner subconsciously welcomes the blame as a form of relief, because they are busy atoning for the same redundant guilt that poisons their psyche.

They belong to the group of people whose behavior we examined earlier. Even if it serves a psychological purpose, ultimately their atonement is ineffective. They are busy trying to save a relationship that is built on imbalance. While the agenda of their partners is diametrically opposed to their own, they endure the abuse in the role of the savior or the martyr. Thus they suffer the self-inflicted agony, which is part of an excuse that keeps them helplessly holding out for the rescue and resolution that can and will not occur.

In order for people with anger and blame that has turned into callous, accusatory, or abusive demeanor to recognize their behavior as unacceptable, they need to first understand what they actually are doing. Then they may be able to open up and experience their own emotional wound caused by unnatural directives. Because of the general amnesia with respect to cultural taboos around this entire subject, the situation is such that this confrontation hardly ever occurs. Unless their behavior is extreme or criminal, they receive very little critical feedback. By and large their anger serves as a smokescreen that perpetuates the offensive posture.

When we point out their behavior as part of an unacceptable or dysfunctional pattern, the majority of the people who fit this description simply refuse to see that any of their conduct may need improvement. Their stance is one of skepticism, repudiation, or dissension serving to enforce and secure their dominance and autonomy. There is no acceptance or any active part in taking responsibility for their actions. They display an inability to dedicate themselves to seeing any truth in what is presented to them. Resistance to considering and acknowledging the issue is still their preferred and only mode of operation. Without the necessary reflection no change can take place in this subconsciously allocated dynamic.

Many people do not display the active projection of anger as a result of resistance to suffering from artificial guilt. Rather than demonstrating some form of emotionally abrasive, mentally cruel, or cynical behavior, they simply have a blunted response to relationships and all emotional aspects of life. This behavior often also is supported by the aftereffects of trauma. The people afflicted are basically feeble, helpless, and emotionally debilitated to the point where they need someone else to fill in the blanks. They will not see their own denial as a lack of emotional engagement.

In this case resistance to unnecessary suffering has turned into an immature stance of oblivious self-absorption and narcissistic expectation. Instinctively or deliberately, they have given up dealing with the unnatural concepts and dysfunctional guilt complex altogether. Their denial translates into immature self-focus, which is supported by a culture that excuses even much worse behavior as normal. The artist who is in love with his own creation to the exclusion of affection for his children is an example of this type of behavior. And so is the mother who, abused as a child herself, is now immersed in her own world of denial, and unable to emotionally give of herself. To the detriment of the child, this dynamic commonly is not recognized by anyone.

In order for this last pattern to shift it is necessary not only to reflect, but also to do inner work in the form of deep and competent psychotherapy. These people first need to learn how to take responsibility for their own emotional reality. Without understanding and owning up to the emotional wounds underlying their denial, they cannot let go of their passive resistance to suffering resulting from the redundant guilt. Furthermore, it is often necessary to address unresolved trauma, and to work it through. The way to change here is through willingness to first accept that there is something that can and should change. But just like in the case of anger and blame, compliance to reflect on their behavior, and then to condone and embrace change frequently is missing.

The person's maturity level, commitment to change, and desire to find their inner truth is very limited or nonexistent. While frozen in helpless, unspoken, and immature expectations, resistance in the form of denial remains their preference. Just as the culturally acceptable behavior of subliminal anger blames in an overt fashion, the impaired behavior of emotional oblivion expresses itself through covert demeanor. When confronted some of the typical responses are distress, portraying the victim's stance, skepticism, argumentative conduct, and denial. Why would they have to change? They question in honest bewilderment how anyone could be so cruel as to criticize their complacency, when they have obviously done nothing wrong.

These people can attract a partner into their life who takes care of them on an emotional level. Only too many people are readily available to look after such grown up children, especially since they are in no way actively cruel. Taking care of someone who seems so helpless is a way of atoning for his or her own underlying pattern of unresolved inadequacy. It also can be a means of feeling in charge. Evidently, this pattern sooner or later backfires. As these people never give of themselves emotionally, their partners end up feeling frustrated. The relationship turns into an emotional battlefield or a graveyard.

The latter two types of contemporary behaviors can exist in combination within the same person. It also is possible to have a joined psychology with dedication to suffering through atonement together with resistance to suffering that generates anger and blame. Any combination is possible, but usually one type of behavior predominates. Relationships are formed in ways that allow these motifs to feed off one another. Excessive guilt, blame, atonement, narcissistic behavior, and victimization are the machinations of the deterioration of modern human connections and communication.

As we have seen, the yielding reaction to psychological guilt stemming from unnatural concepts is one of surrendering, and the assertive reaction is resistance. Surrender takes strength, but the individual often is oblivious to the fact that nothing is gained in the process. Resistance is the denial, skepticism, refusal or unwillingness to act in accordance with this guilt, while nevertheless influenced and motivated by it. This behavior tends to be blind to considerate social action, right conduct, and emotional truths.

For stabilization of these two modes of operation, the yielding response needs strengthening through resistance, and the aggressive response needs softening through surrender and acceptance of weakness. In a world of complementary opposites, one polarity cannot exist without the other. When we actively seek harmony within, our unhealthy behaviors thus far perpetuated are transformed. They yield to a stable accord. Convergence finally wins over habits and conditioning.

Through observing relationships it is possible to recognize these distorted archetypes of modern social behavior. The learned unnatural guilt plays out in all areas of life. We can see the patterns in the sphere of work, intimate relationships, social or political activity, religion, or spirituality. They also are present in the way people regard and treat their own body, or in any setting where an exchange of information takes place. Observing and matching the tangible reality to the characterized behaviors is the first step to heal the underlying causes.

These behaviors are not inherent, but mere attachments, the heritage of the Dark Age. As we begin to use intuition, we can allow the inner eye to recognize the truth without a convoluted or unnecessarily complex rationalization. What is true affects our natural understanding. It reverberates and responds to the unhealthy pattern once this pattern is encountered. Thus it becomes possible to break free from the outdated mold. As a process of separating the natural from the fabricated yet deeply ingrained afflictions, our growing awareness can make them tangible. Evolutionary healing offers suggestions to release them.

Whether we are in a natural relationship to ourselves and the world, or whether we lack this healthy prerogative, the primal forces of evil will continue to haunt human condition in one way or another. It is a basic part of existence within the duality of manifestation. Even during the light phase of the Great Galactic Cycle this phenomenon still exists. In other words, the purging of unnecessary guilt will not eliminate the root cause of evil, but it will definitely help to lessen it. Although it is not necessary to fear the dark principle, it remains a force to always keep in mind as the undermining power that tries to separate us from all that is good and true. Its strength is greatest around the dark peak of the Great Galactic Cycle. This is the time we are urged to leave behind us now.

The powers of creation, continuation, and destruction control matter and consciousness. The concentration of these forces varies according to the phase of the Great Galactic Cycle. Superimposed on time and space the power of creation is most active during the light peak of the cycle, and the force of destruction is prevalent during the dark phase. Preservation on the other hand becomes most significant during the transition times in the middle of the descending and ascending arcs of the cycle. In the descending arc the lack of esteem for care-giving qualities diminished the power of preservation to an exclusively finite resource. The ends that justify the means eliminated true meaning and feeling from the life preserving principle. This promoted the motion of involution from spirit into matter.

In the ascending phase, preservation of the long forgotten, but ultimately true and infinitely valuable, paradigms of caring and conservation leads from involution to evolution. Hence, we now need to become ever more concerned with the preservation of natural laws. These laws are seen in equality of all nations, races, both genders, and all spiritual and religious paths. They are also highlighted in the need for maintenance and restoration of the planetary biosphere. The Great Galactic Cycle helps us to understand these three elemental life energies of creation, preservation, and dissolution in a useful way. By fostering the specific qualities that are necessary to accomplish a timely shift in the big scheme, we ensure gradual rather than cataclysmic change. This is one of the primary applications that illustrate the practical core intention of evolutionary healing.

18. Evolutionary Prescriptions

Cultivating ideals, supporting positive aspirations, and nurturing the desire to do well are essential aspects of life. They help to build confidence and raise hope. It also is necessary to expose the reasons for negativity or despair. Sorrow and anguish arise from mental sickness and spiritual ignorance. Through intelligence, wisdom, and loving acceptance all challenging conditions can be improved. With the vast and invaluably helpful perspective of the Great Galactic Cycle and its practical application to the present time, a new and exciting direction of healing is emerging.

As we have seen, there are three basic responses to unnatural suffering. The first one is dedication or yielding, the second is active resistance, and the third response is passive resistance. Usually these patterns are found joined together rather than in a pure or isolated fashion. More often than not one pattern predominates. It takes experience and practice to successfully identify these behaviors, since they are not always so obvious. As mentioned before, the pattern of passive resistance requires consistent psychotherapy to consciously explore the displaced or denied emotional structure. Provided that this is the only pattern, healing continues of its own volition once the therapeutic course has been completed.

The following directions are medicine in the process of evolutionary healing. The first recommendation is tailored toward the configuration of active resistance to unnecessary suffering due to distorted beliefs or redundant artificial guilt. It is applicable, however, to anyone who desires to move toward the evolution of conscious awareness. The second prescription is for the person who persistently displays the behavior of dedication to unnecessary suffering.

Whenever we are creative in any way, this process is subject to stagnation. The ego is not the source of creativity, which is why it can suddenly dry up. If our ego were in charge, it would be easy to simply continue on this course at any moment we choose to. But this is not the case. The truth is that the Universal Source is trying to create through us in a unique way. If we allow this to come about, stagnation gives way to easy flowing expression. Resistance to the process signifies a need to own and command creativity. This is really not possible. Instead of moving with the Source, the personal will in this case has an egocentric bearing. Hence stagnation occurs to signal that the flow of energy is blocked.

Without alignment with the infinite creative potential our limitations become painfully obvious. Letting go of a domineering will transcends the illusion that true creativity originates from and is owned by the ego. Humbly accepting divine guidance permits the ego's adjustment from identifying with only itself to identifying with the undying soul within. This is not denying any natural process or any personal desire. Rather, it is a masterful collaboration of the finite with the infinite. By listening and trying to understand what life wants to create through us we can contribute to our evolution in a unique way.

Often limitations in creativity occur through mental restrictions. It is therefore important to bring our thoughts into line with the unlimited potential within us. In order to access this unlimited cognizant potential, we need to have a conscious relationship with the Universal Source. The more this relationship is developed, the easier it becomes to tune in with what it is the Great Spirit intends to create through us. This is not only important when being creative in our thinking, but also when interacting with other people. Redundant patterns of behavior are easily identified as such if they have a repetitive negative outcome, or when they do not mutually benefit all persons involved.

Our behavior is defined by the boundaries of our thinking. To understand our behavior requires that we invest energy into knowing ourselves. It is a function that frequently is neglected. People with a pronounced resistance to the aforementioned pattern of unnecessary suffering that is coupled with anger think that as long as their agenda is met, other people's view and situation is irrelevant. This opinion leading to selfish and exploitative action clearly lacks accurate reflection. It also is due to the mentally restricted belief of separateness. An imbalanced "win/lose" situation is always caused by lack of alignment with other people's power and intention. If on the other hand the objective is mutual advantage, we discover new ways of interacting that never have been experienced. The following questions are appropriate in any interaction: "How do I come across?" "How can I facilitate the other person's needs without sacrificing my own?" "How does this make me feel in return?"

Moving the focus from self to others eliminates the need to succeed at the expense of someone else, even if this is not how it is perceived by the ego. It seems difficult to let go when success has been apparent. The compulsive desire to come first regardless of the consequences is caused by the ego's resistance. The ability to see that the perceived route to success at the expense of someone else is naturally wrong, and no true success at all requires a desire to improve. Conscious effort needs to be applied to change the existing pattern. This can occur only if the person is willing to see the world from a different perspective, and is able to let go a little from his or her mental restrictions of separateness. The realization that we are all connected and that there is always a more inclusive solution will turn the "win/lose" to a "win/win" situation. A noble pursuit of improving relationships does not only help others, it directly enables the evolutionary journey of one's own soul.

When dedication to suffering is prevalent the individual compulsively atones for the redundant guilt. He or she previously set up a dysfunctional matrix. Depending on the circumstances, someone else may benefit temporarily through being the benefactor of such behavior. Even so, in the end there is no advantage to this either. Maintaining an excessively self-effacing stance will sooner or later cause anger, resentment, and unhappiness. The individual who compellingly atones is not meeting his or her own needs. This produces a deep sense of frustration and inner emptiness. As elaborated earlier, this person will therefore end up creating crisis.

Because there is either no conscious awareness of the pattern or a strong compulsion to maintain it, resisting this behavior is just as difficult as in the above case. These people need to develop trust and love in themselves, in life, and in the Universal Source. By taking one step at a time they will gain the urgently warranted confidence to leave their emotional vacuum behind, and to proceed in a healthier and happier way. Until they have established this inner strength, they require compassionate support and respectful guidance from others. They need to feel that Goddess loves them, and that other people love and respect them. Gradually these people will come to the inner realization that they actually love and respect themselves in their own imperfection. This insight can then extend to feeling worthy of their own, other people's, and God's love. How this process unfolds is different with each person.

Often the above steps toward evolutionary healing are not enough. The subconscious mind may require additional alteration relative to the imprinting that conditioned the psyche to needless atonement. Since these behaviors prevailed over many lifetimes, they are deeply ingrained in the psyche. Frequently they cannot be accessed and changed using the conscious mind and willpower alone. Practical steps therefore need to be taken to alter the subconscious mind.

Even if it is counterproductive, self-consistency creates security. During the evolutionary process resistance to change is everpresent. The pattern of self-effacing behavior due to unnatural atonement and dedication to suffering has become second nature. What underlies it is the perceived necessity to survive. Because we had no awareness or opportunity during past incarnations, no choice in this matter existed. A desire to change and to be of service may have been the second motivating dynamic. This demanded a strong personality. Strength to sacrifice therefore is not what is missing in this case.

The conscious mind already has gone through perpetuating cycles of analysis, self-effort, and improvement without finding another solution. This is why this case often requires additional steps. The secret is to develop the skill to assert oneself in a healthy and balanced way, which can be achieved only through subconscious reprogramming. Due to the distorted cultural beliefs and customs it was necessary to deny the personal needs, and instead develop a subconsciously subservient mentality.

The human organism is designed to survive. Cultures now are changing worldwide, and what is necessary to survive also changes. Consequently, once the age-old conditioned link between survival and submission is broken, new behaviors can emerge naturally. Over many lifetimes this pattern has been deeply ingrained through sheer necessity. It cannot be canceled without employing a method that targets the immediate mechanism of survival itself. Simply knowing and intellectually understanding these dynamics is not enough. Moreover, cultural change is slow; most environments still support the old ways. Despite the changes that are underway, this redundant behavioral mode is constantly reinforced and supported.

The following instructions have helped people to alter their subconscious self-effacing behavior. With the right jumpstart it is possible to set healthy responses in motion again. The changes are deep and remarkably profound. The best way to do this is through autosuggestion during sleep. The ego is the carrier of the conditioned self-image. During sleep it is temporarily suspended, and can therefore not fight new input. This is when the subconscious mind is receptive to alternative suggestions. During the waking state the ego rejects these suggestions. This is not because they are not true or not useful, but because the ego is used to perceiving itself and life in a certain preconditioned habitual manner.

The way to accomplish subconscious reprogramming of the mind is by way of self-hypnosis through developing a set of positive affirmations. This is followed through in a process of altering all negative imprints into positive ones. Every negative and self-effacing statement must be erased and substituted by a supporting affirmative declaration.

Begin with a piece of paper and a pen. Divide the paper vertically into two parts. Focus on recalling every negative statement that has ever been expressed toward you. Their origin does not matter; maybe a teacher, parent, spouse, friend, or unknown. Simply write all of them down in the left hand column of the paper. This process may take a couple of weeks, or even a month. You may go through one or 20 sheets of paper. The right side of the paper always stays empty. It is important to follow the inner process of recalling, making them verbally deliberate, and writing all of the negative statements down. At some point this process will feel complete.

Now develop the antidote to these negative messages. In doing so, write all positive counterparts on the right side of the paper. Keep in mind that any negative word is to be omitted. For example, if you have in the left column the sentence: "I am ugly." You want to develop the polarized statement by rephrasing it as: "I am beautiful." Do not say: "I am not ugly." This would subconsciously reinforce the word "ugly". When all the negative statements have been canceled in this way, forget about them altogether. From now on the only thing that matters is the right column with the affirmative statements.

The next step is to record these personalized affirmations on a blank tape while leaving a silent leader of at least 20 minutes.

Record in your own voice all the positive declarations once through, no more. You may want to get a longer audiocassette, such as, for example, a 90-minute tape. This way you can begin to record after 30 minutes or more. The reason for leaving a blank leader before the recorded statements is so that you can fall asleep undisturbed. The point is for your mind to hear these statements only after you have fallen asleep. You may also use a digital recorder, which lets you select the time of the playback. This way you can have as much time before your affirmations as you need to be sure you are in a deep phase of sleep.

The sound of one's own voice is most comforting. It should reach the brain through the right ear. The right ear is connected to the leftbrain, which is where the self-effacing subconscious messages of the past are stored. Here is where the alteration takes place. Play the tape at a low volume, just loud enough to hear it. The affirmations need to play only once per night. It requires the consistency of a minimum of four months of repetition, however, to permanently alter the subconscious imprinting. No night may be left out. If there is a break in this routine, you have to start counting from scratch, and go four months from that point forward.

It is not unusual that some kind of error occurs with this playback system. Very interesting things can happen. Tape recorders break, get misplaced, batteries run out, or an unexpected trip will interfere with the newly established routine. Often it is the ingrained messages that are desperately fighting back to keep the subconscious mind ensnared. Thus, the ego subliminally will attempt to undermine this venture. At this point sabotaging the nightly playback routine in some covert way is really the last chance to fight change. Understanding this dynamic will help to persevere under adversity.

Once the subconscious mind has been retrained successfully, it is still a matter of consciously applied effort and consistency to effect the desired changes in all areas of life. With habitual actions the predisposition of self-effacing behaviors yet needs to be broken in the realm of conscious tendencies. Many situations will arise where proclivity to fixed routines is an automatic response. These outward trends still attempt to reinforce the undermining attitude that already has been released within. If the individual relies solely on the newly established subconscious program, these emotional habits triggered by outer circumstances can yet persist to be a major stumbling block.

In the beginning stages after the successful completion of the tape, overriding the new inclinations happens unnoticed. Instead of acting in tandem with the inner healthy focus, reverting back to the old familiar mode of handling a situation can still occur automatically. This is especially the case when new circumstances create additional stress and insecurity. If not checked and redirected, the old mode of thinking and acting will undermine the subconscious healthy affirmations. The same danger also exists in situations where an unfulfilled desire provokes the individual through temptation. It is important to examine and analyze any conscious desire or motivation that gravitates toward the ingrained behavior. "Why do I want this?" "Am I just acting out of an indiscriminate habit?" and "What will be the outcome of my planned actions?" These are some of the necessary questions to ask when confronted with familiar circumstances and temptations that tend to trigger the dysfunctional pattern. If these questions are asked with detachment and discrimination, the firmly established subconscious underpinning will support this fresh direction unfailingly.

It is natural that to launch a new habit takes energy, discipline, and concentration. This is why it is important to consciously substitute healthy behavior for the detrimental tendency. With time and practice the healthy matrix will become second nature. Then the conscious thoughts and actions match the newly established subconscious configuration that naturally promotes self-esteem and healthy assertion. Evolutionary healing occurs through this process.

Exertion toward spiritual growth is moving consciousness from separation to unification with the Source. We can achieve this through connecting with other people. Any relationship conducted in the spirit of altruism will augment the principle of unity. If we want others to be happy and fulfilled instead of thinking exclusively of ourselves, we are making an effort of being one with them, and with the Source by extension. The important thing to remember, nonetheless, is that what we want for others cannot be done at the expense of our own comfort. With this in mind, putting others first can bring enjoyment and satisfaction unparalleled by any self-focused action.

For people who are compulsively sacrificing themselves for others or for a cause they perceive worthwhile, this paradigm truly cannot work until they heal. These individuals first need to get reacquainted with a positive self-image and learn to be there for themselves in a healthy way. The likelihood of encountering this redundant atoning and sacrificing dynamic is elevated for many people who honestly are trying to spiritualize their life. This is because of the subconscious memories and religious conditioning their soul has been exposed to in this and in previous lifetimes.

On the path to healing it can happen that such individuals become excessively assertive, self-focused, or controlling. They have now reached the opposite polarity. In the original position there was no conscious concept of self-confidence and self-preservation. But now their consciousness is engaged in predicting any possible danger to the extreme. Every aspect of life is calculated, planned, and mentally overseen. The weak ego has grown stronger, and strategies for self-assertion have been developed to the point of wanting to feel invincible. There is no imprudent spontaneity, no naiveté; everything is controlled and efficient, really rather overefficient. This compulsive phase in the evolutionary healing process is an inability to accept fear and limitations as inseparable aspects of life. If they are seen as such, and if the reasons for this phenomenon are understood correctly, this phase can be minimized.

Life's innate fears and dangers prevail in their own fashion despite acquired skills and efficient strategies. Now letting go of the newly earned control is needed. It is important to realize that there will always be limitations and vulnerability. To become truly impeccable the way life appears to be in this phase is simply impossible. Thus the realization ultimately prevails that the individual never will have absolute control over life, that life happens with or without his or her cooperation. Now impeccability means accepting life and its unexpected turns with fear as an ally that helps to signal inherent danger.

Over-reactive behavior and excessive need for security and control also can be associated with an apprehension of losing the newly found sense of self. With time the individual will experience that in fact this recovered healthy sense of self cannot be lost. When pointed out respectfully and with the appropriate reassurance, this specific concern will diminish and finally vanish all together. True self-validation is accomplished through service to others and society, and through seeing oneself as a creative vehicle of life's intentions. No one can know what lies ahead, nor do we have a method of controlling the future. The important thing is to keep an open mind, and to have a willingness to do the best we can do. Improving step by step means to accept the inherent imperfections of life. While knowing that the value lies in the effort, evolutionary healing can proceed. It comes about through self-esteem, the seasoned skill of self-preservation, concerned forethought, and finally the spiritual wisdom of letting go into the uncertainties of life.

When it is not reckless or for lack of involvement and responsibility, jumping into the abyss of the unknown is a powerful skill. Sacrificing our limited ego awareness enables consciousness to expand. Ultimately we are meant to submit with unrestricted devotion to our destiny. Then there is no place to go to, because we already have arrived. This is not denying any natural process or any desire.

Fulfillment comes through surrendering to what life wants to create through us. Our immediate situation is the only reality. It contains the key to the past and to the future, and teaches us to dance with life. In every moment we are asked to become the best we can be, to apply and share what has been gathered during our highly individual experience. Beyond perfection, fear, self-preservation, and limiting control life is calling for the attainment of our true purpose. This purpose is to live with maximum affect, but without attachment.

19. Trauma

More than half the population now suffers from some form of unresolved trauma. We are currently faced with such a high percentage because of the distorted ways human life developed in cultures that are out of alignment with life's natural directives. For example, many people accumulated massive unresolved trauma because of their compulsive atonement to artificial guilt. Sometimes it is exactly through trauma and the way it is creatively resolved that evolution proceeds in intended and profound ways. In these cases the trauma serves as a catalyst for growth. More often though trauma is not dealt with in a productive way, but rather ignored or misdiagnosed. This can become a major roadblock on the evolutionary journey.

In order to facilitate its healing we need to first understand what trauma is exactly. Furthermore, it is vital to recognize the importance of addressing unresolved trauma, and to know how to identify the symptoms of post-traumatic stress. Understanding how its consequences alter a person's normal behavior and comfort level are essential cognitive skills. To affect healing for self or others or both, we must know that there are ways in which trauma can be resolved.

Trauma is a severe physical, emotional, mental, or spiritual disruption caused by stress or shock. The traumatic event itself can take place on any level, such as, for example mentally. Yet the effects will not be restricted to the exclusive experience within this one plane of existence. Physical trauma manifests through circumstances such as accidents, injury, torture, rape, degenerative diseases, or birth defects. Emotional trauma includes abandonment, misapplied trust, and psychological or sexual abuse; experiencing catastrophic events of a personal, collective, or environmental nature such as an earthquake, a flood, war; or the sudden death of a close person. Mental trauma consists of unexpected or abrupt changes that alter the reality of the person, various psychological disorders, stroke, epilepsy, and diseases of the brain. Spiritual trauma occurs through the loss of faith, values, or beliefs; intense disillusionment; and in rare cases invasion and possession by an unwanted spirit. These traumas can have a continual effect on all levels of existence.

Trauma typically impacts the entire organism through a chain reaction. The effects linger on past the time the actual incident occurred. The delayed stress or shock is experienced as irrational responses, behaviors, or beliefs that do not reflect the present life circumstances in a realistic way, and is known as post-traumatic stress syndrome. The person may be overreacting in situations that do not call for such an extreme response. Or he/she could be frozen and totally passive when a normal reaction would be appropriate or necessary. Such irrational behavior patterns indicate that some unresolved trauma is underlying the observed abnormal response or lack thereof. In more severe cases trauma can cause serious afflictions such as psychosis, schizophrenia, displaced hysteria, bipolar disorder, psychopathic behavior, extreme paranoia, claustrophobia, agoraphobia, intense rage, pathological lying, and disassociate behavior/personality disorder.

Post-traumatic stress syndrome is an instinctive desire for healing, although often is not recognized as such. The delayed stress response is the soul's attempt to relive the effects of the trauma in order to complete the experience that was too overwhelming at the time it occurred. It is as though unresolved trauma split the life force into moving forward and backward at the same time. Through successfully reliving the circumstances that caused the energy currents of the life force to fray, the stress can be released.

Often the individual does not consciously remember the event or series of events that caused the trauma. Due to its severity and threatening nature the traumatic incident itself is suppressed. The psyche is unable to cope with what is happening and therefore refuses to acknowledge the shocking reality for the sake of survival. The only possible way to preserve the integrity of the organism is to keep going as though the traumatic event never occurred. All the same, the delayed stress originating from the trauma continues to create symptoms, while the causative dynamics lie buried within the subconscious memory of the individual. They are suppressed and therefore create distorted responses.

The subconscious mind is accessible and responsive without the person's discerning awareness. As an extension of the brain the nervous system continues to react to the traumatic event as though it were a reality like the one consciously perceived by the senses. The individual's system deals with the stimuli it receives from the brain, but there is a lack of awareness that the symptoms are related to a past event. Emotions come up that seem to be exaggerated or out of context. The person affected by an unresolved trauma also may offend or startle other people with a behavior that is extreme or imbalanced. Yet there is no circumstantial factor present that would explain these disturbances. They remain utterly enigmatic to self and others.

The subconscious memory of an unresolved trauma produces symptoms that can range from being less than desirable to rendering the person in some way dysfunctional. Instead of seeing them merely as negative or unwanted occurrences, it is necessary to acknowledge these disturbances and to understand their link to the past. Thus they become helpful hints on the path to health and wholeness. This is why the blunted or otherwise unnatural response occurs in the first place. It is a sign that a split took place in the integrity of the body/mind continuum, and that the effects are not integrated. When a rock is thrown into the still water of a pond it causes waves. Similarly the lasting effects of a trauma persist to disturb the integrity of the entire organism. In some instances they do work themselves out on their own. Often the symptoms are severe enough, however, to cause distressing effects. It is then important to consciously work on recovering the memory, and thus unlock the traumatic event. Often the same responses occur with similar stimuli. This can be a clue to the nature of the unresolved trauma.

When the actual content of the trauma can be remembered in a supportive therapeutic environment, the person will experience the natural responses that previously were blocked. Their imprints lived on in some form despite the fact that they were no longer conscious. They remained manifest in the psyche as an idea or an emotional complex, as subconscious memory in the brain, or as cellular memory in the body. This disruptive energy pattern kept running through the circuits of the nervous system and through the wireless anatomy of the electromagnetic field in and around the body. Once the connection is made and the actual trauma is remembered, the suppressed psychological patterns and emotional armoring related to the traumatic circumstances may be released. Then the defective energetic and electric wiring of the subtle body and the nervous system repairs itself.

Even if a traumatic event has never been suppressed, the shocking reverberations keep on negatively affecting present behavior. Post-traumatic stress disorder is a disease many soldiers face after returning from war even though they remember what happened there. Other examples of situations that cause post-traumatic stress are severe illness, serious accidents, witnessing domestic or random violence, incest, rape, or a hostage situation. Sometimes denied and suppressed, other times remembered, the psychological or psychic disturbances that the trauma created have a life of their own. Through working on the memories and allowing the emotional reactions to impress and transform the psychological traits, this delayed stress reaction gradually can be integrated into the personality.

Depending on the severity of a trauma, the symptoms of delayed stress may not dissipate entirely. Nevertheless, they change when the trauma consciously is worked with. A small pebble and a massive rock thrown into the water both cause commotion, but the pebble creates no more than ripples, while the massive rock forms big waves. With the pebble it will take less time for the ripples to disperse and for the surface of the water to resume its stillness. Likewise, the length of the recovery process varies depending on the severity of a trauma. When an effort has been made at integrating the remaining symptoms, the individual may be able to function quite adequately. Rather than being like a runaway train, the delayed stress syndrome becomes manageable. When seen from a larger perspective, the subsequent healing commonly is more extensive than what can be encompassed with a limiting view of instant gratification. The potential long-term benefits are always well worth the effort.

Our subconscious memory is not restricted to present life events. It also contains the information of all lifetimes previously lived. This is why it embodies an immense pool of information. An unresolved traumatic factor from some incident that occurred in another lifetime may be hidden within the subconscious mind. Its memory can be reawakened by some present event. Sometimes this retraumatizes the person. With specific personality disorders the delayed stress may be present from birth. In this instance the post-traumatic stress disorder is operative even without any particular provocation. For example, this can be the case with autism or childhood schizophrenia.

In other circumstances a particular incident may trigger something about an unresolved traumatic past life event. Factors such as divorce, a new job, a move, or a new relationship suddenly can alter someone's outer reality. The newly emerging disruptive symptoms may or may not be manageable. In either case, these symptoms are challenging to the normal functioning of the organism. The activated delayed stress response stands in the way because of the limitations it contains.

Some form of inner change that modifies the psychological reality of the individual also can prompt post-traumatic stress. In this situation the cause is inherent in development and is related to a new phase of life, such as puberty or middle age. The trigger also can be initiated through illness, psychedelic drug use, regressive therapy, or even through the development of a metaphysical skill. Meditation, for example, directly mobilizes the evolutionary force. On occasion even meditation can trigger a previously hidden past life trauma whose aftereffects need conscious healing. Whatever the cause may be, the nervous system recalls the information via subconscious memory, and symptoms emerge that have never been experienced. Because it has not been dealt with in a satisfactory way, the trauma is yet to be resolved relative to its psychic content. The long-standing or newly emerging symptoms relate to the subconscious unresolved past life trauma. The delayed stress syndrome creates a disturbing mental attitude, emotional response, or spiritual belief that prevents the person from moving forward.

In the case of reactivated past life trauma, there is a need to remember and release these aspects. It is possible to understand and consciously facilitate the integration of past life information. Healing occurs relative to the driving thoughts, emotions, or beliefs that hold a disruptive negative charge. If the memories or emotions are expressed in some way, it is usually possible to understand them. Once they are worked with in some fashion, they can be integrated. With this the individual owns and consolidates what has not been otherwise accessible. New ways of responding to the old stimuli finally are permitted to emerge. This will metamorphose the limitations for the person to move forward.

The Great Galactic Cycle's current phase offers us an explanation about why more people experience this last type of trauma. The redundant patterns of artificial guilt caused much unnecessary suffering. Many individual souls have lived lifetimes where they have accumulated massive trauma. Collectively as well as personally the turning point has arrived where everything is changing. For those who are sensitive to the fated changes, the resolution of unresolved trauma triggered by some present cause is a vital part of their evolutionary healing journey. Provided it is applied in conjunction with the right cognitive skills, this approach offers a practical alternative to limited psychological models and available allopathic treatments. Often the traditional healing models do nothing but delay an individual's inevitable evolutionary steps. When a person's system is ready to purge trauma, suppressing it with drugs or models that label the disturbing symptoms of delayed stress as abnormal or diseased is countertherapeutic. Of course medication is necessary when normal functioning is no longer possible. Otherwise, and frequently even in these cases, people should seek additional and more comprehensive healing to what ails them.

There are specific methods that can be utilized in order to unlock and consciously remember personal traumatic events, especially also those resulting from past lives. Spontaneous recall may occur of its own volition through situations and circumstances that resemble those of the traumatic event. If a person has the tools of recognition the disturbing symptoms may dissipate.

Provided that the practitioner's focus is tuned into the evolutionary healing model, energy bodywork also can lead to spontaneous call back of suppressed trauma. It is a highly effective method if the client is receptive to this approach. Initially the surfacing cellular memories may be restricted to the physical and emotional levels of the client's sphere of perception. Hence the practitioner's cognitive guidance is needed in facilitating these experiences. As trust in the organism's innate wisdom is gained, uncovering further layers will follow. With continued work the fully conscious recollection of the entire trauma is sure to emerge. Sometimes the resolution can occur within a single session.

In the process of healing trauma there are many useful methods, hypnosis being a well-known technique. An unusual but sometimes also effective means is gong therapy. In cases where a partner is available, the use of a sacred sexual practice such as tantra can be a valuable medium too. This method is especially well suited to heal sexual trauma.

Trauma occurs also on a collective level. There is political, socioeconomic, philosophical, as well as environmental trauma. The delayed stress syndrome involves all these levels. A fundamental need for restructuring is becoming ever more obvious. In order to be free from outdated political, socioeconomic, as well as philosophical structures, many nations are undergoing massive changes. It is apparent in many places such as, for example, the revolutions in Eastern Europe, the fall of dictators in South America, and the ongoing tumultuous changes in the Middle East. Religious war is an example that illustrates both the need for as well as the resistance to philosophical change.

The social and economic imbalances in the United States are increasing the evolutionary pressure and the need for rebuilding. Collective and individual trauma takes place via the channels of disillusionment, psychological futility, hopelessness, and depression. As difficult as this may be, it nevertheless is vital in creating a climate of reflection. Eventually and irrevocably this will alter the deteriorating socioeconomic environment along with the tendency for corruption within the political structure. It will enforce the need for personal involvement of the citizens, whose complacency and indifference gradually created a reality that is dangerously oblivious to what is occurring. The consumer's decadence and the illusion of the American Dream will have to give way to a practical social democracy. Not unlike the Roman Empire a couple of millennia ago, it will otherwise fall prey to an unexpected enemy and perish.

In order to allow for the inevitable changes that are bound to happen, the planet and all nations will continue to undergo progressive change. Due to the inherent subconscious need for consistency and security, this process of necessary modification is subject to much resistance. Just as it occurs on a personal level, because of fear of insecurity, collectively too the signs for unavoidable change are ignored or repressed for various reasons. The suppressed symptoms create pressure that increasingly intensifies. Sooner or later change can no longer be resisted. Depending on the strength and duration of the resistance, disastrous events will lead to more or less intense trauma.

We now have overpopulation, terrorism, astronomical budget deficits, along with declining social services and unaffordable health benefits, merging corporations, the formation of cartels that hold the wealth of more than ninety percent of the nation, and religious groups trying to dictate their one and only way to know God. Preemptive war also has become a phenomenon. Leaders worldwide, and especially those of some of the most affluent nations, do not seem to have the basic desire to overcome their self-interested motives. Their focus is nowhere near the reality of what we are facing. These phenomena necessitate cataclysmic changes. This in turn will create increasing numbers of traumatic conditions.

The imbalances in all areas of life are becoming ever more critical. The effect the ruthlessly exploitative human behavior has on the natural environment reflects back on us. This impact certainly is traumatic on a collective level. The fact that our way of life is no longer synchronized with the natural directives of existence has psychological and spiritual implications. Although they may not be conscious, those implications can be quite traumatic as well. Many modern disorders, ailments, and maladies originate from the trauma of living a life that is fundamentally at odds with natural principles. More and more people are suffering from depression, free-floating anxiety, obsessive or compulsive behaviors, sleep disturbances, sexual dysfunctions, abuse, as well as an array of other maladies.

At the present time the entire planet is in a state of trauma. We are observing how natural disasters are progressively increasing. Pollution of the atmosphere, contamination of waterways and the entire ocean, as well as ground poisoning through illegal or unregulated dumping of toxins, and the depletion of trace minerals from the soil through imbalanced monofarming, all are signaling the syndrome of trauma.

Global warming already is causing massive changes to the coastlines. Some of the Pacific islands are in the process of sinking completely. Extreme weather conditions are monitored globally. In many areas they result in much damage. Increased radiation due to the degenerating ozone layer impacts all life on the planet as living things mutate to adjust to a changing environment. Simultaneously the impaired human immune system has weakened, and has increased our susceptibility to contagious diseases. The HIV virus is but the first microorganism that managed to adapt in a way that has so far proven to be nothing short of perilous to most people.

The delayed stress responses of planetary trauma eventually will reach a critical point, at which time none of these phenomena can be denied, ignored, or underestimated any longer. Evolution will continue to be preceded by involution until a necessary natural balance has been reached. Obviously this will happen with or without human cooperation, and the resulting trauma for humanity will be quite severe. The choice of whether we are going to cooperate and move toward the necessary realignment with nature, or whether we want to continue in our delusive ways is ours, at least for a little while longer. The Piscean prophesies of apostle John's apocalypse in the New Testament does not have to become a reality. It is a vision of warning for the times following the dark peak of the Great Galactic Cycle. Ultimately humanity will come to the realization that we are all in this experience together, and that we had better start acting one for all and all for one.

20. Kundalini

In the human body Kundalini equals the physiological substance that causes evolution. It is created by and contained in a gland that is located behind the sacrum at the lower end of the spine. The Kundalini gland is atrophied in most humans living on the planet today. Over the centuries this gland has been forgotten and is therefore no longer part of anatomy as taught today. Most people have never even heard of it. Similar to trauma and its syndrome of delayed stress, awakened Kundalini can produce symptoms that typically are misdiagnosed or inexplicable. Consequently, it is important to recognize these symptoms for what they are. Once the circumstances and conditions that trigger Kundalini are identified, it is possible to find the individually relevant accurate context within which to place and integrate these symptoms.

Many people possess no independent impulse to develop as individuals outside of the expected norm. In a blind urge for security and conformity they simply adapt to the mainstream pact of society. In this segment of the population, Kundalini, the physiological substance of evolution, is nonactive. In this we can see once more the result of thousands of years of conditioning that emphasized fabricated ideas and manmade premises, the basis of which were not centered in natural living. Accordingly, natural behaviors and reactions became curtailed and substituted with artificial ones. To fit in and comply with the contemporary social conditions, people automatically restrained their inherent emotional, sexual, and physical responses. Within the consensus of society the need to behave in a conformist way resulted in subconscious repression and subsequent distortion of these aspects. The entire organism was negatively influenced and thus prevented from working to its full capacity.

Because it is dependent on the natural functioning of the human organism, the Kundalini gland degenerated. It therefore no longer produces the substance that facilitates evolution and ceased to play an important active role in human development. Of course individual development is still taking place. It primarily arises through slower modes of transforming limitations such as, for example, reflection or learning that involve the mind and the senses.

Development through the activation of the Kundalini substance is a fast, deep, and very effective way of growing past the limitations of past habits and redundant conditioning. As we transition toward the Age of Aquarius, the reactivation of the Kundalini gland is bound to occur. For people who have developed their individuality past the mainstream of society, there is a potential for Kundalini to be stimulated already at this present time. Among them is a small segment that is willing to try out new methods of learning and growing. Since this involves the emotional body, it is still restricted to those who are relatively undaunted to confront their security needs and who are willing to alter their habitual behavior. During transition times such as the one we are in, inevitable social restructuring occurs. Standard values, customs, and rules will undergo major changes in all cultures. With this the reactivation of the Kundalini gland can take place for a larger part of the population. Human evolution will accelerate, which is necessary in order to adapt and keep up with the environmental requirements for survival.

Particular biological rhythms correspond to certain age periods in the life of every individual. They initiate opportunities for developmental changes. During such periods a person may suddenly get in touch with subconscious memories that he or she never accessed. The same is true for latent talents that at key points of inner development can emerge unexpectedly. Mental and emotional evolution also can be triggered by cataclysmic events such as the loss of a loved one, a divorce, relocation, or a change of employment. The resistance that normally keeps the organism at a locked level of functioning is worn down during such times. If the person is keyed into the expansion of his or her conscious awareness along with any of the above changes, it is possible for the Kundalini substance to become activated in the body.

When the Kundalini substance is released into the system, it changes any cell that needs alteration or healing. This tends to produce symptoms such as tingling, burning, sensations of coldness or heat, and numbness. Even temporary paralysis of a limb can occur. The symptoms are almost impossible to diagnose even by the most experienced of allopathic physicians. Old injuries long forgotten may suddenly reappear. Body cells have a memory, which can be triggered by the release of Kundalini. This is not referring to scar tissue and its related symptoms, but rather to pain or sensations that have no physical explanation and are not chronic or constant. Nevertheless, there may be cells that have not sufficiently healed from an injury or illness. The released Kundalini substance finds these cells to be in need of improvement or alteration, hence the symptoms. If such symptoms persist for an extended time, they will most likely catch the person's attention in a negative way. He or she may become concerned and seek medical advice, needless to say, to no avail.

To make matters more complicated; memories from a previous life or lives can be triggered through the release of the Kundalini as well. This may result in physical pain or certain physical manifestations pertaining to injuries, accidents, violence, or any other traumatic incident from a life or lives long forgotten. Since the creation of the individual soul, all events that occurred throughout all the lifetimes have been recorded. Some of these events leave unresolved issues or trauma the soul desires to work out at a later date when cultural norms have changed sufficiently to make a resolution possible. The latent information of the event pertaining to these unresolved past life issues is stored as cellular memory in specific cell arrangements in the body, as well as in the subconscious long-term memory in the brain.

The release of the physiological Kundalini substance activates the cellular memories. Simultaneously it also stimulates the flow of the conscious life force. Therefore, the experienced symptoms–provided they are not too painful or disturbing–can simply be allowed to run their course. This is hardly possible if the person is puzzled and frightened by them. The body will become tense, and this tension results in impaired circulation, which is counterproductive to the cellular exchanges that need to complete themselves. Due to the unnecessary emotional stress, a negative biofeedback loop arises that produces even more tension.

The preferred scenario is that the individual is able to retrieve long-term memories pertaining to the experienced symptoms by way of intuitive direction. Although the veil that separates the present from past lives normally obscures the actual event, over time its nature can be sensed. The individual consciously connects the memory of the past incident to the symptoms in the body. Then a spontaneous recall becomes part of the healing process. It facilitates the integration of the needed physical, physiological, and emotional components. In preference to resistance and denial, which only results in tension, the process is followed through to its end. The conscious integration of these dynamics moves people along their evolutionary path.

On a psychospiritual level Kundalini energy possesses inherent intelligence. Once it is active, it has the power to metamorphose limitations within consciousness. Thus it also initiates necessary liberation from past conditioning. The active Kundalini energy can bring emotional memories of past life circumstances to the surface. A certain external situation or some specific event in the present can set them off, and this is a sign that something has not been fully resolved. It is important to take these emotions seriously and to process them accurately, to enable the release of outdated limiting habitual mental/emotional patterns or spiritual beliefs. What has come before is no longer relevant for what is about to happen. Purging of ingrained behaviors and obsolete beliefs is vital.

When examining the interplay of spirit and matter in the context of human evolution, we find that Kundalini energy plays the role of growing awareness. With its separating impulse of individuation from the Source into creation, the path the energy takes leads from the subtler frequencies of the causal plane of consciousness and ideas to the astral plane of life force and feelings, and finally to the denser vibrations of the physical body. Cosmic life energy flows into the system through the medullar chakra at the base of the skull, from where it continues along the spine downward through the cerebrospinal centers to the root chakra at the base of the spine. How exactly the conscious life energy "steps down" from the subtler to the physical level is extremely complex and beyond the scope of this book.

In ordinary living much energy is used for sensory perception that feeds matter-bound-awareness. The general tendency for the life energy is to move toward the lower centers in the spine. These centers are related to the basic instincts of survival, procreation and egocentric activity. The focal point of most people's attention via sensory impressions is concentrated on these aspects of life. The higher centers govern realization of the subtle realms above and beyond physically manifested conceptions. They are associated with the ability to detach from physical impressions and responses. Through this detachment an awareness of the higher self–the soul–can be gained.

Developing human consciousness requires reversing the downward flow of cosmic life energy through the subtle spinal centers, and thus raising this energy from the root chakra at the base of the spine toward the crown chakra in the cranium. To reverse the flow of conscious life energy and to guide it toward the higher centers, specific methods can be employed. The methods themselves are timeless and taught by enlightened teachers and saints. Many of these scientific techniques have been forgotten in the long process of conscious decline related to the Great Galactic Cycle. Even so, some enlightened teachers like Jesus, Buddha, or Bhagavan Krishna emerged during the Dark Age and passed on such techniques. A select group of devoted individuals learned and disseminated their teachings.

With the use of scientific techniques it is possible to refine and redirect the superfluous energy not needed for the proper functioning of the lower spinal centers. This energy can serve the evolution of human consciousness. The subtle channels of the astral body hold and govern the flow of energy that regulates feelings and emotional responses. Once the energy flow becomes restricted, a blockage occurs. Over many generations the life force has been tied to the frequencies of the lower chakras. Nevertheless, repressing any function of the senses, desires, and actions involved with the world is not possible. Even from an energetic point of view it will cause stagnation and distortion.

The conditioning of behaviors related to societies that do not honor life's natural directives trained people's mental, emotional, and psychological responses. This prevented them from realizing any of the obstructed natural dynamics. Reversing of conditioning patterns is the necessary step backward that frees the flow of cosmic life energy to access the underlying potential for evolutionary progress. Clearing the passageways increases general vitality and sets the stage for the reversed energy to rise toward the higher chakras.

This process of reversing the flow of life force in the subtle spinal centers or chakras is what in some schools of yoga is called raising the Kundalini. This channeling of energy gradually expands human awareness. Kundalini is then no longer a physiological substance, but rather the subtle essence altering consciousness from ordinary perception to the realization of the soul as the true driver of the human vehicle. Thus Kundalini as a phenomenon has both a physical and a metaphysical component.

It is primarily for individuals who actively seek to spiritualize their life that the metaphysical aspect of the rising Kundalini energy comes about. This is the result of an active intention and effort to advance through meditation and through disciplines such as yoga, tai chi, tantra, or any other genuine sacred practice. When this second type of Kundalini experience occurs, it lifts the ordinary consciousness that alternates between pain, pleasure, indifference, and a false sense of peace to the awakening of authentic calmness, nonattachment, and bliss. It brings about a dispassionate realization that consciousness is the only thing that is permanent about our existence.

There also are ways to raise the Kundalini energy through sexual practices that have a spiritual focus. Human beings possess the ability to cocreate with the Universal Source through sexual union. Through the past millennia of declining conscious awareness this application has nearly been forgotten. The vital essence contained within the sexual fluids of the male and female body is very potent. Its preservation and discerned use is particularly important. Energetically, this vital fluid also contains the entire karmic information of the soul. Through sexual intercourse all karmic data is passed on to the partner. Along with other important factors, discernment in choosing such a partner is therefore a key issue. Unbeknownst to most people, promiscuity and haphazard choices greatly weaken the psyche. They can lead to a sense of not knowing what issues are one's own, and what has additionally been taken on from another person to work out. The result is confusion, disorientation, and stagnation or backtracking on the evolutionary path.

Sexual energy possesses a tremendous force. With specific methods it is possible to harness this energy and use it for sacred purposes. The conjoining of two people whose focus and commitment is to help one another grow spiritually accelerates their evolutionary journey. Instead of being exclusively centered on pleasure, sacred sexual practices shift the intention toward creating soul union. Through constant and steady eye contact the two partners lock their mind into refined perception. This cocreated awareness also has healing power, including the resolution of past life traumatic events.

This type of sexual union is vastly different from practices that aim at heightening physical pleasure or try to create longer lasting or more intense orgasms. As a matter of fact, with sacred sexual ways orgasm rarely occurs at all. Although this does not mean denial of pleasure, concentration is on the soul reflected in the partner's eyes, not on bodily sensations. The climax of spiritual sexual union is the reversal of one's life energy toward the higher chakras. Thus the vital fluid is retained and its potency transmuted through the awakened power of Kundalini. The preserved energy of love, passion, and deep soul connection continues on past the sexual act; it is carried into daily life through embracing each moment and every activity, no matter whether important or seemingly insignificant. Instead of weakening the organism, this type of sexuality increases natural vitality on all levels. It teaches through simple means to cultivate refined love in a sacred way. In preference to climax and recline, the quintessence of lovemaking sprawls over all waking hours. The abundant satisfaction gained through this grants deep relaxation during sleep.

In times to come human consciousness will once again expand to astral and causal energy perception. Next to many other sacred customs rooted in the wisdom of eternal truths, natural sexual practices with a spiritual focus will receive favorable attention. We can already see this proclivity in the present wave of energy and vibratory healing methods. With the increasing evidence of their beneficial results, these methods are gaining more popularity and recognition. They will turn out to be the norm rather than the exotic exception, because the old ways will no longer work. Eventually this will compel ever more people in the direction of accepting the subtle realities underlying the appearance of matter and form. They will thus come to embrace a naturally spiritual purpose. As the galactic forces are once more in the process of evolving toward the light of conscious awareness, Kundalini will be accelerated on a more collective basis. This is especially vital during transitional times such as the present shift to the Aquarian Age.

In summary, we can say that any incident involving the activation and release of the biochemical substance of Kundalini occurs in connection with certain key events or activities. These may be triggered by outer circumstances, or simply through biological junctures universal to the progressive unfolding of life rhythms. When Kundalini is stimulated unresolved trauma can resurface, causing great stress. Other triggers of Kundalini are related to the psychological development intrinsic to the subjective experience of individual reality throughout a human life span. And last, but not least, the refinement of life energy into Kundalini energy is a direct result of any sincere seekers' spiritual efforts.

21. Basic Principles of Healing

Healing means becoming whole, moving toward greater balance, increased vitality, and a positive outlook on present circumstances as well as on the future. Sometimes the right physical treatment along with simply resting and giving the body an opportunity to recuperate is all that is necessary. At other times healing involves deeper changes. The disease becomes a subconscious habit, and it takes much energy to liberate the mind from this. For example, psychological healing from childhood wounds encompasses learning to let go of a past that no longer supports the current conditions. Through a form of conscious reflection the person gains insight that there has been a counteracting tendency to habitually re-create past circumstances and behavioral patterns. Active involvement can effect the necessary changes. It also takes courage to face and surmount the feelings of insecurity, uncertainty, and anxiety that new choices and behaviors often bring about.

This same dynamic also operates in regard to physical healing. We tend to get used to thinking that an illness or injury has to run its predetermined course. Once we know we are ill or wounded we act as though this state had sovereignty over our being. This restricts the mind from directing the cells of the body. Although it is often too difficult to change our thinking, there have been many accounts of doing just that. This usually is accompanied by unencumbered and natural lightness, as though it all happened by itself. It is faith and the alignment of personal will with divine will that can heal us instantly on all levels.

Health is a function of inner radiance. Without this inner sparkle a person can eat nutritionally balanced foods, lead a relatively healthy lifestyle without much stress, and exercise well. Nevertheless, if there is no inner happiness, there is no actual vitality within the system. Inner radiance develops along with positive thinking and establishing a conscious connection with the Source. Since the Source is the supreme intelligence that guides everything, a conscious relationship enables us to develop deeper meaning for our existence. Doing the things that bring us true fulfillment also recharges inner liveliness.

Basic Principles of Healing

Healing inspires us to move forward with positive energy. The desire to heal, to become whole, is simultaneously a desire to realize our unlimited potential. Ultimately, this is our birthright, the reason for our existence in the first place. There can be no genuine wholeness without merging our individual conscious awareness with the cosmic consciousness that created us. Consequently, all healing in the end is spiritual healing. Either consciously or subconsciously, it enables us to open up and connect with the Source.

Through intuitive inner knowing, conditioned beliefs that block healing may be confronted and released. When shrouded by unnatural concepts and guilt, an individual's consciousness is kept in a nonempowered and codependent state. Discharging thoughts that are not in harmony with the natural principles of life must happen first. This impacts on the emotional body, and realignment with actual inner experience can follow.

Although healing is essentially a spiritual process, it can take place on three levels, the physical, the mental/emotional, and the spiritual. Each of these planes of existence has different requirements and conditions. All three are of equal importance and have to be addressed respectively. Physical disease traces back to a weakening of the life force. There are many reasons for this. Sometimes it relates to the nerves. As they get weak and frayed they can no longer perform their tasks adequately; the electrical current is impaired, and the organism begins to malfunction. This can be caused by mental or emotional stress. In other instances the weakening of the life force is due to organ dysfunction because of wrong living, for example, overeating or unhealthy eating, lack of exercise, overindulgence in drink or sex, and stress. A holistic lifestyle coupled with moderation and some practice of self-management, such as yoga, will increase the flow of life energy and facilitate the overall vitality of the system.

In times to come mental healing will reach great efficacy. The inherent intelligence of the mind created all the cells of the body. When mental concentration and personal willpower are aligned with divine intelligence and cosmic will, human beings can cocreate with this infinite force. Since the body heals from within, it is possible to convert basic cells to obey the mind that may then use these cells to create new body parts such as inner organs or limbs. This is how people healed during the Spiritual Age. Lucid consciousness enabled them to use their mind to effect changes in the body with cells that retained a plastic state. In this state these cells were not subject to genetic specialization but rather impressionable by the governing mind to build according to its dictates. During the dark phase of the Great Galactic cycle healing became fragmented. In sheepish obedience people's mental power succumbed to externally imposed restrictions. Thus the disease consciousness of the materially constrained mind forgot its omnipotent sovereignty. Eventually it presumed the delusive limitations of physical existence to be the only reality.

Even at the present time people whose mind is strong in discrimination can on occasion effect mental healing with the use of reason. These individuals are able to control their body by shutting out the thought of disease in their mind. Since they are not accepting the apparent reality of illness or injury, their body can heal from within. Other people are impressionable by imagination. Their mind follows and willingly submits to a suggested idea. They heal in the relief experienced from such a proposition. The different forms of consciousness people are endowed with stimulate different energies. Therefore, it is essential to know whether an individual is strongwilled, imaginative, or primarily governed by reason. The appropriate mental healing method is chosen accordingly.

Psychological maladies are disturbances such as fear, anger, failure consciousness, lack of self-esteem, worry, egotism, and lack of initiative or confidence. Many of these afflictions also are healed with mental control. Affirming the opposite polarity by meditating on that concept often is very effective. For example, if someone is troubled with fear, concentrating on courage will bring the balance. If anger is the issue, seeking peace and ignoring the anger rather than acting on it can also be helpful.

If there are unresolved emotions from childhood or past lives, then just focusing on the counterpoint will not be sufficient for a cure. The remedy is found by exploring the emotional content. In this way the attitudes or beliefs that generated these emotions are discovered, understood, and put into perspective. Healing takes place through this process and through the subsequent mental realignment with positive thoughts that validates the person's experiences and present circumstances. Since thoughts and consciousness are the only permanent aspects of human existence, infusing the system with positive thoughts supplies unlimited access to life energy, which is available at all times. Positive thoughts are the pipeline to infinity, the true source of all healing.

Spiritual ailments primarily are caused by blindness to the divine purpose and meaning of life. They include imbalances such as lack of purpose, intellectual superiority, dogmatism, satisfaction with the material side of life, indifference, and ignorance of natural life directives. Their healing entails developing concepts such as truthfulness, generosity, humility, contentment, and respect for all life. Cultivating an awareness of the oneness of all life increases these virtues.

For restoration of balance and vitality on these three planes of existence a certain amount of faith, cooperation, and surrender is necessary. If physical and especially psychological and spiritual healing is to be truly successful, acceptance of the concept that we are all accountable for the realities we create and experience is important. This can become an inner felt sense only when the conditioning patterns of the past are transmuted by self-determination. The old thinking patterns and models of behavior were permeated by codependency, guilt, and by a sense of victimization, powerlessness, and passivity that translated into "Why is this happening to me?" Self-reliance on the other hand is the necessary basis from where the evolutionary healing process takes place. It creates a shift in awareness, so that another question can be asked: "Why did I need to create this situation for myself?"

For healing to occur it is necessary that we learn to make the right choices in terms of the existing situation, related circumstances, and predicaments we face. In the case of evolutionary healing, real change arises with this consistent approach of making new choices in the presence of familiar circumstances and inner quandaries. As long as out of emotional habit, fear or insecurity the familiar path is chosen again despite rationally understanding that it is wrong, there is no change. Life will continue to present this challenge of right choice making.

Sometimes it is necessary to travel back along the path until we reach this pivotal point. Compulsive action for trepidation, insecurity, lack of self-reliance, or emotional conditioning will always bring the same old results. Therefore it is necessary to transform the core issues.

Faith is also a critical element in the healing process. To cultivate a field of corn it takes both potent seeds and fertile soil. The same is true in the field of healing. The healing power of the practitioner is necessary as well as the faith and responsiveness of the client. Only a fully enlightened individual has the power to bring about healing without the faith and conscious cooperation of the person to be healed. With acute or chronic conditions the element of faith is emphasized. Believing that one can be well physically, emotionally, mentally, and spiritually is much more important than the actual present state. Faith is intuitive conviction that carries a person through adverse conditions. On a soul level it is this inner knowing that perseveres in the face of circumstances that contradict the individual's beliefs. Faith therefore needs to hold steady through the stormy seas of these challenges.

Healing is a science and an art simultaneously. It has in its core an ability to let go of trying to control whatever is happening or not happening. The result is the steady development of natural insights instead of preconceived expectations. It often is necessary to work out a strategy that targets the underlying causes resulting in the symptoms at hand. This strategy is different for each person, and can include all levels of existence. In this way a new sense of composure is established within consciousness. Patience, tenacity, willpower, and trust in the process all are part of this healing path.

The healing progression has a dynamic of its own and needs to be honored and respected. It comes into view for each person in a different way. There are patterns and similarities, but the underlying reasons for the manifestation of blockages, disease, and imbalances vary with each case. They make sense only when understood in their original and highly individualistic context. Unless the deeper causes are acknowledged, they will continue to produce symptoms. Moreover, real change and permanent healing is possible only when we have a genuine desire to do whatever it takes to affect this healing. Self-determination and will to cooperate with the conditions life presents are the prerequisites that demonstrate this desire. Taking responsibility for our own healing course is necessary, because it provides proof of sincerity and commitment to accepting the fact that we are all responsible for the realities we create. If we created imbalance and blockage, we can also create their removal.

Many blockages in people of Western societies are related to the emotional body, as this is the area of life that is most suppressed. Acceptance does not happen in the rational mind alone. Not a single facet of existence can be suppressed, or further imbalance will result. Of course this is an ideal concept, and life is practical and imperfect. Evolutionary healing aims at the resolution of suppressed emotional content through a step-by-step procedure leading to restoration of the natural equilibrium.

In terms of trauma resolution the appropriate guidelines are vital. Although subconscious memories can be useful in unlocking trauma, remembering such content needs to be done with moderation and be kept to a minimum. Unless they are directly linked with an unresolved trauma that is clearly blocking us from moving forward, trying to recall subconscious memories is utterly countertherapeutic. Even while working on such traumatic memories it is really important not to get preoccupied with attempting to understand the complexity of past or past life circumstances. The focus outside of the immediate healing session or spontaneous recall needs to remain on the present moment and the current conditions. If we started to remember much of our past lives we would not be able to fulfill our evolutionary intentions in the present. This is why we do not consciously remember all these lives and the details and events therein.

Once a soul is fully liberated, there are no boundaries that separate any aspect of total reality from one's own reality. Personal consciousness expands into the sea of cosmic consciousness where everything is present simultaneously. Obviously this is not a state a regular human being can bear without losing his or her mind. Many mental disorders relate to subconscious or unconscious data that is indiscriminately being poured into consciousness, and thus overwhelm the individual to the point of dysfunction. Ordinary limitations of consciousness are therefore as necessary to the healthy mind as the walls and roof of a house.

It is the task and duty of evolutionary healing to define the margins within which the work of recalling and understanding past life events is useful. Employing the proper perspective ensures that this can be done without any real danger. In the case of necessary past life recall, factual memory may not even be required. As long as we can grasp the content of a past life scenario in a story or parable, its intuitive truth is realized. Many memories merely serve to supply us with the background in which we place the emotions, unnatural guilt, redundant habitual patterns, irrational fears, rage, and so on. Spiritual psychology seen from the perspective of the Great Galactic Cycle's alternation of spirit and matter-bound human consciousness allows the soul to continue its journey through time and space. It can thus receive the required evolutionary healing within appropriate boundaries.

The future of healing is with efficiency rather than with codependent, repetitive, and seemingly endless consultations. This does not necessarily mean that the healing process will be fast, but it will be self-governed with occasional effective sessions to reaffirm and guide our evolutionary needs. An invaluable tool in this practice is a method that aids in understanding the underlying dynamics and intentions of the soul for the current life. Evolutionary astrology is a tool that accelerates the comprehension of soul issues. A firm grasp enables a practitioner to map out the reasons why the client is experiencing the specific circumstantial life predicaments or physical or psychological symptoms, and why he or she became ill or imbalanced in the first place. Because the soul's desires and evolutionary needs are essentially unconscious, a viable method of gaining insight is invaluable. It allows our soul wisdom to become conscious. As we experience the moment at the crossroads of choice making, it bridges the tension between past and future.

To receive healing we are often also asked to give. Letting go of an aspect we no longer need makes room for new growth. Bad habits are the enemy of progress. If we cannot let go of compulsive action that threatens our well-being in some fashion, we are not able to move forward. Tying loose ends happens before new beginnings can commence. This does not mean that one has to be perfect, but definitely aware. Awareness grows through owning one's inner reality instead of acting it out in some fashion.

Under normal life circumstances prayer alone may not be sufficient. Despite great efforts bad karma of past lives can limit the mental patterns in subconscious circles of negativity. When immediately following meditation, however, prayer becomes highly effective. Meditation is one of the best ways to ease the evolutionary healing process through growing awareness leading to spiritual sensitivity and divine inspiration. With developing concentration the rational mind is balanced with the intuitive side of the brain. Through intuition we are guided to understand natural life directives, which enables us to take the next step. When no conscious awareness is available, the rational mind is obviously at a loss with information that pertains to subtler levels, or another time and place such as past or future. Therefore, the information needs to be accessed by a different route. Intuition is always tuned in with solutions, because it relates to the super-conscious mind. Developing consciousness can therefore never fail to provide us with the needed information. This acquired positive quality fosters clarity to perceive and realize truth and love within existence. Inner happiness becomes the new ground that ends all sickness born of negativity.

22. The Age of Aquarius

The Piscean Age generated beliefs that were rooted in artificial concepts and religious dogmas based on superiority and inferiority. People were conditioned to follow rationalizations given by authority figures with ulterior motives of greed and power. The common populace learned how ultimate direction came from a source of authority outside of them. These directions contained unnatural guilt as a method for control, thus generating blame, resistance to suffering, cruel behavior, urge to dominate, desire or need for submission, useless sacrifice, and perpetual crisis. This dysfunctional psychology also resulted in a preoccupation with the past. It concluded in history repeating itself, instead of history setting an example from which to learn and move forward.

In the Great Galactic Cycle's phase of expansion, the Age of Aquarius is going to be a very important turning point for humanity. Liberation from the past is written in the stars of this constellation. That liberation from the past is of utmost importance; it is related to the fundamental changes that are now manifesting on our planet. In this time old patterns are coming to conclusion and new formations are randomly emerging. It requires the courage to let go of familiar yet outmoded ways of thinking, behaving, and acting. We can greatly benefit from opening our mind and from accepting new thoughts that enter our consciousness, as this consciousness is now trying to expand.

Many great teachers, sages, and saints over time have pointed out that all real knowledge is free. What we need we already possess within. All we really have to do is to simply intuit the truth. New belief systems that are in harmony with natural life directives can thus emerge. It becomes ever more important now to follow one's own heart, and to stay connected to a simple lifestyle that respects the oneness of all life.

An important phenomenon of the approaching Aquarian Age is acceleration. The world population has doubled in the past 50 years, and is likely to do so again within the coming 50 years. This clearly shows the phenomenon of acceleration on a global level. People of any age also experience it individually as a sense of time speeding up. A day seems to pass as though it were merely a couple of hours, weeks fly by like days, and at the end of a year it is hard to believe that the entire cycle of the seasons is already beginning to repeat again. This experience can cause free-floating anxiety, an uneasy sense of time running out, or a feeling that there is never enough time. Without understanding the natural dynamics of this occurrence, it generates a great amount of unnecessary stress. If on the other hand an awareness of this phenomenon is gained, the focus can shift to what its actual reason and intention is.

We all have certain ways of thinking, acting, and behaving that are intrinsic to our individual nature. From a neurological point of view all data, whether pertaining to sensual impressions, actions, feelings, or emotional states, are transmitted from the nerves to the brain. Depending on many factors this information becomes organized, and eventually is directed toward intellectual or intuitive comprehension. The order in which we classify information is unique. Over time this classification develops circuits and thought channels in the brain. As the electric energy prefers to run along the already-established paths, these neurological routes become deeply ingrained. The pathways are then used automatically, and it is almost impossible to break them. Hence the thoughts, actions, and behavior pattern themselves grow to be habitual and fixed. It takes reflection, concentration, and repeated use of willpower to detach from the deeply ingrained patterns.

Electricity is the basic medium the brain and the nervous system use for transmission of all information between the nerve cells. Through electrical impulses traveling along the sensor and the motor nerves, messages and information are carried between the body and the mind. All functions related to feeling, intellect, and will also are dependent on electrical transmission. The Age of Aquarius also relates to electricity, which is the basic vehicle cosmic life energy uses in the manifested creation. An increased amount of electric energy strengthens our life force. The additional supply of energy may be employed to evolve the nervous system, the very core of which is the brain.

At present the cerebral cortex has developed only approximately 10 percent of its actual capacity. With the Aquarian Age approaching rapidly, the amount and the strength of electrical impulses are raised. The higher amplitude and accelerated pace by which nerve impulses in the brain are transmitted pilot the formation of new connections between the synapses of the already existing dendrites. These nerve cell connections develop new pathways that lead to new habits of thinking and behavior. The number of possible connections between brain cells is greater than the number of atoms in the universe. As there are approximately one hundred billion nerve cells in the brain, the potential for fresh connections is nearly unlimited.

With this perspective it becomes apparent that the potential for the evolution of human consciousness may burst the boundaries of our present imagination. The brain's growing capacity arising from this evolutionary leap is likely to lead toward a holographic consciousness, in which past, present, and future are perceived simultaneously. Thus the Age of Aquarius heralds possibilities beyond the scope of a conditioned mind, which is still struggling to cope with the new challenges in old ways. As they interfere with the sense of continuity and wholeness, the conditioned patterns can no longer be sustained without causing logical incongruities. In this holographic matrix the existing limitations of thinking and behaving are transformed. With this type of consciousness redundant manmade paradigms have no chance of surviving.

The Aquarian energy supplies the human organism with an opportunity to evolve the brain through the medium of accelerated electrical stimulation. This evolutionary process is still, however, in its preliminary stages. Instead of using the additional energy in an organized manner, the nervous system and the brain tend to get overloaded. This augments the stress level and aggravates modern lives already too busy and preoccupied with excessive complexity. Without the right guidance and understanding these changes are difficult to integrate. This is obvious in the array of symptoms that has befallen people of today's world. The majority of the population experiences some difficulties related to stress. If furnished with the above knowledge, it becomes possible to accept some of these symptoms as signs of the time. Instead of seeing them as an epidemic that has to be fought and suppressed, we can accept them as the forerunners of an immense prospect for change.

Many people notice thoughts that seem to occur out of the blue. Puzzled or frightened by these arbitrary thoughts that emerge without a logical connection, they wonder whether they are losing their mind. They end up doubting themselves in bewilderment or they reject these thoughts unsuccessfully. But despite the fact that they do not make any rational sense, it is best to simply allow them to exist on their own. Thus these random thoughts can become components of a new way of thinking. From this perspective they are nothing but partially established neurological pathways. Even if such random thoughts are only feeble first attempts at connecting the wires in an evolving brain, this approach removes the compulsive need to get rid of the symptoms. Letting go and understanding these dynamics permits acceptance of arbitrary thoughts as fragmented pieces of information pertaining to a more evolved and powerful consciousness. We eventually will succeed in putting this consciousness, like a jigsaw puzzle, together.

Sleep disturbances are another common modern complaint. Many people find themselves wide-awake in the middle of the night. There is no specific explanation, but out of regular sleep their brain suddenly works in daytime mode. Most individuals unsuccessfully try to continue their interrupted sleep. With this phenomenon too another tactic reduces stress and aggravation. Why perceive this state of wakefulness as annoying, when it is simply a sign of the times? The initially unwelcome disturbance can be viewed as an opportunity to catch up on some reading, for example. It is likely that before long the system will thus settle down. This taxes the nervous system far less than self-created irritation or medical prescriptions. Moreover, knowing how to fall asleep quickly in the middle of a busy day is a feature that will come in handy in the approaching times. This is a good motivating factor in learning to tune into one's inner world through some meditative discipline. An evolving brain calls for a changing lifestyle and the acquisition of new skills.

Depression is one more major grievance many people express at this point in time. It is natural to consciousness and only needs to be treated if it interferes with the normal ability to function. When the status quo is no longer satisfactory, we find it necessary to draw our attention inward so we can reflect on our life. Although this process of reflection my not be conscious, the resulting depression is often the sign that our system is recognizing that our patterns must change. The values and beliefs of the concluding Piscean Era are no longer congruous with contemporary existence, neither do the old ways of thought and behavior fit the mold of successful coping with the demands of an emerging new way of life.

Depression is the barometer of functionality indicating that it is time to change gear. This is especially true for the crossroads we have reached regarding the broader perspective of the Great Galactic Cycle. With the turning of the tide past its darkest peak, the new values and emerging qualities can no longer be ignored or suppressed. When the times change radically, as is the case now, our thinking and feeling nature needs modification. Just as it is natural to wear the proper clothing for every season and occasion, every Age requires a new mindset. For evolution to proceed, the existing limitations call for a metamorphosis. Resistance to this process of necessary change and adjustment may well lead to depression. Depression is then merely an indication that adaptation has not yet taken place sufficiently. Once an understanding and acceptance of these psychological implications is achieved, we can consciously work out the resistance. This approach is in alignment with the important message of liberation that the dawning Age of Aquarius conveys.

The Age of Aquarius

Willingness to accept impermanence, imperfection, and uncertainty as part of reality builds trust in the inherent intelligence of life. Since the cycle of becoming is part of the divine evolutionary plan, aligning ourselves with its inherent wisdom provides us with the resources to take the next step. Above and beyond the conditioning of the past we may thus become more comfortable with our destiny and our authentic nature. The core of this process is a gradual shift from preconceived artificial notions of how things should be to natural values. Through embracing the challenge of change we let go of the past and begin to build a solid foundation in the present moment.

The approaching Aquarian Age clearly signifies planetary change. The Western mode of operation is undoubtedly on a collision course with nature. As a direct result of human exploits, the Earth is getting ready to rear her head. Although cataclysmic events are apparent and to a certain degree inevitable, the degree to which they are likely to manifest is dependent on immediate collective and individual human choices. If humanity is able to cooperate with the inevitable changes, they may not be as disastrous as foreseeable at this point. Our most immediate task is the effort to maintain the integrity of the planet's biosphere. Concentration and cooperation on a global level is vital so the planet will continue to support human, animal and plant life.

Increasingly more people are waking up to this plea. In the crisis and tension of the present these people are hearing the call of the Earth. They resonate with a distant memory of cataclysmic global events still embedded in the collective unconscious. The dawn of the Aquarian Age is suggesting a unification of all people to align with the laws of nature in an effort to face and cope with this ever-increasing threat of surely approaching natural catastrophes. The people who are tuned in with these changes sense them as a gloomy premonition. Will we use the faculty of discrimination to stop wasting precious resources, and share those resources with all others in a balanced way before it is too late?

All the dynamics that were in operation during the Piscean Age are coming to a head within a short amount of time. The purpose for humanity is to bring these dynamics to completion and to move on to more suitable ones. History shows that during the culmination of any Era this usually does not happen. The tendency is to repeat the same mistakes. Most people simply do not have the ability to detach and to see things for what they truly are. Rather than allowing for evolution to take its course, they blindly follow the existing direction. Thus, history repeats itself.

Approximately 25 percent of the population has learned in varying degrees how to detach from the stagnated values of the consensus. This segment of the population speaks for the need of humanity to evolve beyond the present. The current predicaments keep repeating themselves under the leadership of the blind. The necessity to objectify and discriminate the most important issues is therefore becoming urgent. People who are willing to move on from the past harmonize with the ideas that are going to be relevant for the coming two thousand years. They have a sense of the dawning Aquarius Age. This Age also correlates to entirely different ways of being social.

In a movement of humanitarian effort toward global unification, this segment of the population urges the masses to get beyond the present state of inertia and disharmony. Many are eager to endorse the beneficial qualities of attunement with natural life principles. Others are devoted to promote the eternal truths of our spiritual reality. While clearing their subconscious mind from conditioning patterns of the past, these people regain their long lost inner freedom. Many of them are committed to doing all they can to stop the cycle of repetition from happening. It is thanks to movements like this that we have new developments in history.

Now is the time to begin building our future in a joint effort by embracing the necessary adjustments to help steer toward decisive changes. This approach is not about perfection, nor is it fathoming an ideal existence without challenges. It is simply an appeal to a way of life that is natural in allowing and expressing all aspects of one's own true being, which includes actions such as respecting the validity and inherent rights of all life. The Western system is likely to collapse or at least very fundamentally change. How grave this will impact human life depends on what decisions we make now.

23. At the Crossroads

Release from the swing of polarization occurs through becoming all knowing, all seeing, and all one with the Source. The expansion of consciousness into omniscience demands conquering all fears and attachments. It also means embracing the physical, mental, and spiritual laws of life. Within these laws all aspects of existence are equally necessary and valuable. Life and death, destruction and creativity, good and evil all arise from the same Source. The struggle to stay above board with benevolence, love, and kindness makes us stronger. Just like the emerging butterfly gains enough strength through flexing its wings to finally break free and fly away, our relentless endeavors will eventually free the soul from its earthly journeys.

The cosmic interplay between spirit and matter takes place in the arena of human consciousness through cycles of awakening to the natural spiritual directives and inhibition of awareness leading to materialistic deterioration. This ebb and flow of consciousness caused by the Great Galactic Cycle spurs evolution of human awareness. Natural truths become evident through progressive cognizant growth. The final objective is each individual's realization of the soul as the only permanent reality.

Arriving at the crossroads during critical evolutionary phases, we must make necessary choices. Whether we are faced with cataclysmic events or gradual change is often a direct result of these choices. In either case the irreversible consequences bring about the turning point. The reason for wise decisions becomes apparent in the reality of natural principles, some of which have been elaborated on in this book. The crossroad calls attention to the past decisions, present choices, and immanent consequences we are given a chance to ponder before it is too late. The intention was to supply sensible answers. The guidelines can be used along with one's own experience through observing and correlating in actual life the principles elaborated here. I hope that it will generate a practical mindset for the intense times to come. The provided direction also supports the process of becoming and supplements understanding with any type of holistic healing work.

In the manifested universe spirit created soul, and soul in turn created ego. This is so we know who we are as independent beings. There is no individualized identity without ego. The interplay of spirit and matter allows us to use our physical being to act, create, and learn. If spirit were perfect, it would not have needed to create anything. Life is the manifested evidence of the Source's desire for the metamorphosis of limitations. The notion of perfection within earthly existence is therefore a myth recently created by cultures that have lost their connection with the natural roots of existence. In these cultures the unavoidable confrontation with life's inherent imperfection became linked with guilt and the need for blame.

We have seen how desire is the binding component between the physical, astral, and causal bodies. With the soul being bound by these three encasements, all desires need to be worked out before it is free to exist or be merged with the Universal Source. Therefore, we cannot suppress, deny, or neglect any worldly desires on our evolutionary path. Instead it is vital to make these desires conscious, and to find ways that lead to their realization. Only then can the ultimate last desire to be all one with the Source find fulfillment.

Transcendence ties the cycles of life and death to the wheel of immortality. Following the natural spiritual laws of existence means to worship every action and every relationship. It includes the discipline of first asking ourselves how our own actions will mutually benefit others rather than exclusively ourselves. If someone neglects his or her own well-being in this process, this is still a transgression against natural directives. Embracing an inspirational belief system that affirms life facilitates this process.

The cycles of spiritual awakening and materialistic decline elucidate how deeply and in what ways these trends of consciousness make or break the natural relationship with the Source. Spirit is absolute and therefore abstract and difficult to relate to. It is natural for human beings to relate easier to a tangible figure, such as a male God or a female Goddess. Regardless, it is important to be conscious of the limiting attributes we project along with this image. Attachment to finite existence brings out the trickster to torment our being. It highlights what scares us to make our choices dependent on a finite outcome or a concrete goal. The invented punishing God who rules with conditional love reflects this dynamic.

Evil denies transcendence, immortality, and inspiration; for humans the price is bondage. Since malevolence has its own intelligence, it is necessary to increase our awareness to keep up. If worry or fear, for example, obscures a project or one's livelihood, then the principle of destruction is given more meaning than it deserves in this specific context. Worry will obstruct a goal through catering to negativity. It ruins personal willpower to persevere and takes away vision, confidence, and inner security.

The individual will yield to weakness, doubt, and fear. This is vastly different from necessary change, which also contains an element of obliteration. Yet in this case the obliteration merely makes room for new growth, it is not causing senseless damage. Just as death is followed by rebirth, life is constant change. It only takes away what is necessary. The change of the seasons is an illustrating example.

Where are we now, how can we liberate from re-creating a past that no longer serves the present evolutionary requirements, and how can we move forward? Evolutionary healing views the personal as well as collective human and environmental implications from the perspective of consciousness, energy, matter, and spirit. On a personal level it helps to guide the soul's journey through endless lifetimes of chasing earthly desires to the ultimate sanctuary of spirit. In order to map out which desires are necessary to fulfill, we need to know whether we are focusing our attention in the right place. The tension between past and future as experienced in every moment of existence is the crossroads we are facing with all our choices in life. Do we understand the past, are we acknowledging the future, and can we empower ourselves to make the changes necessary to thrive in the present?

Evolution is the inherent pull and supplication of life toward advancement. By removing resistance and aligning ourselves with natural directives, change can take place without cataclysms. When we allow the Source to guide our thoughts and actions through these directives, no obstacle can stop the creative power. This is augmented during the ascension toward the Spiritual Age. Although it is still in the far distant future, we are unalterably headed in this direction. Knowing that human consciousness gradually is expanding enables us to tune into our unlimited potential. This will help lessen many personal, collective, and global imbalances.

At the Crossroads

As a final contemplation let us ponder the reason for the accelerated increase of the world population from the soul's perspective. The intense hastening of human births points to the fact that these souls all wish to come in and participate on the world stage at this time. The turn of the Ages holds a promise of quickening evolution for each individual soul. Remember, in the end it is the strength gained in the struggle to break free from its chrysalis that determines the butterfly's successful flight. Collectively this time also calls for extraordinary measures because of the imminent planetary changes. Being here now means to witness and contribute in some form to the important crossroads of choices. Could we perhaps see the presence of all these souls as a reminder that it is the effort toward love and cooperation that matters and not necessarily the outcome?

Your feedback is welcome.

I invite you to share your comments regarding the material of this book. Feel free to contact me also in case you would like me to give a workshop or lecture in your area. Please send your email to feedback@earthlit.com.

Katharina Wehrli

Author's Services

In her private practice Katharina Wehrli offers soul healing and evolutionary coaching sessions both in person and over the telephone. She also teaches classes on this subject. For more information please visit her website at www. earthlit.com.

Printed in the United States
36397LVS00008B/13